a field guide to using Visual Tools

David Hyerle

Association for Supervision and Curriculum Development
Alexandria, Virginia USA

Association for Supervision and Curriculum Development
1703 N. Beauregard St. • Alexandria, VA 22311-1714 USA
Telephone: 1-800-933-2723 or 703-578-9600 • Fax: 703-575-5400
Web site: http://www.ascd.org • E-mail: member@ascd.org

Gene R. Carter, *Executive Director*
Michelle Terry, *Deputy Executive Director, Program Development*
Nancy Modrak, *Director, Publishing*
John O'Neil, *Director of Acquisitions*
Julie Houtz, *Managing Editor of Books*
Jo Ann Irick Jones, *Senior Associate Editor*
Stephanie Justen, *Proofreader*
Gary Bloom, *Director, Design and Production Services*
Karen Monaco, *Senior Designer*
Tracey A. Smith, *Production Manager*
Dina Murray Seamon, *Production Coordinator*
Barton Matheson Willse & Worthington, *Desktop Publisher*
M.L. Coughlin Editorial Services, *Indexer*

Printed in the United States of America.

s5/00

ASCD Stock No. 100023
ASCD member price: $19.95 nonmember price: $23.95

                    Library of Congress Cataloging-in-Publication Data

Hyerle, David.
    A field guide to using visual tools / David Hyerle.
        p.   cm.
Includes bibliographical references and index.
"ASCD stock no. 100023"—T.p. verso.
    ISBN 0-87120-367-7
    1. Visual learning. 2. Constructivism (Education) 3. Thought and
thinking. 4. Critical thinking. I. Title.
    LB1067.5 .H92 2000
        370.15'2—dc21   00-008213

04 03 02 01 00   10 9 8 7 6 5 4 3 2 1

A Field Guide to Using Visual Tools

Acknowledgments

As you look through this book it is easy to see how many people have offered up their best thinking on visual tools for me to share with you. I appreciate the efforts of all of the students, parents, teachers, administrators, researchers, and expert consultants who are bringing these new tools to a new generation of learners. I also thank the folks at ASCD who have brought enthusiasm and hard work to shaping this *Field Guide*, especially editors John O'Neil and Jo Ann Irick Jones.

Popping up throughout this text are the ideas from one who has coached me from afar for so many years: Art Costa. His insights into thinking, reflection, assessment, coaching, and processes of change provide a grounding upon which I could build this work. I know how deeply Art has influenced me because often in moments of reflection, when I turn to consider alternative views, I think, How might Art have approached this problem? Thank you, Art, for being my coach.

Over the lifespan of bringing this book from initial sketches to the final edits, I have been most grateful to my wife Sara for striving to keep us sane (successfully) while taking the lead in guiding our son Alex in his preschool years. And though I have never taught Alex how to use visual tools, the moment of inspiration for me to *keep on writing* came when four-year-old Alex came running into my writing studio with his first map, yelping, "Look, Pappa, I drew a Bubble Map!" Thank you, Sara and Alex, for giving me this opportunity to share these maps of the mind with others in the field.

Preface: "I See What You Mean."
A Visual Glossary

As the Sufi parable teaches us, our capacity *to see* problems as only two-sided, as dichotomous, often prevents us from seeing and thus entering multiple points of view. By carrying around this metaphor in our language and thoughts, we tend to see people as individuals on "the other side" of an idea or conflict, rather than as they truly are. Conceptual metaphors, and this particular metaphor of *seeing*, are a foundation for everyday life and influence how we feel, think, and make sense of the world.

This book is about visual tools, which show patterns of thinking, and how they help us and our students make sense of the world, communicate better, and become lifespan learners. This mapping may help us to understand how the metaphor of "seeing" is the foundation for and central to the success of visual tools. This metaphor "grounds" visual tools in everyday classroom language. Figure P.1 is a map of some of the everyday uses of the "seeing" metaphor.

This mapping of metaphors is partially based on the work of George Lakoff, professor of Linguistics and Cognitive Science, University of California–Berkeley. For many years he and his colleagues have conducted cross-cultural research in the area of conceptual metaphor. His landmark study, aptly titled *Metaphors We Live By* (Lakoff & Johnson, 1980), reveals the centrality of metaphor to cognition, language, and everyday living. Lakoff's work integrates a wide range of cognitive science research and philosophical inquiry into a new framework for understanding human cognition, experience, and action.

As shown, this metaphor does not stand alone, overlapping with other modalities and spatial/physical relationships in the world. As you link these terms and add your own from everyday life, notice the overlapping of visual and spatial metaphors. For example, "perspective taking" draws from standing in a certain position and then seeing from that "point of view." This is one way that painters, photographers, writers, and other artists gain new perspectives and represent in*sights* in everyday life.

And, as we shall see in this book, our students gain insight into their own worlds when they begin to apply visual tools, look up, and say: "I see what you mean."

A Sufi Parable

To see "both sides" of a problem is the surest way to prevent its complete solution because there are always more than two sides. (Shah, 1972, p. 56)

Preface: "I See What You Mean." A Visual Glossary

vii

FIGURE P.1

Everyday Uses of the "Seeing" Metaphor

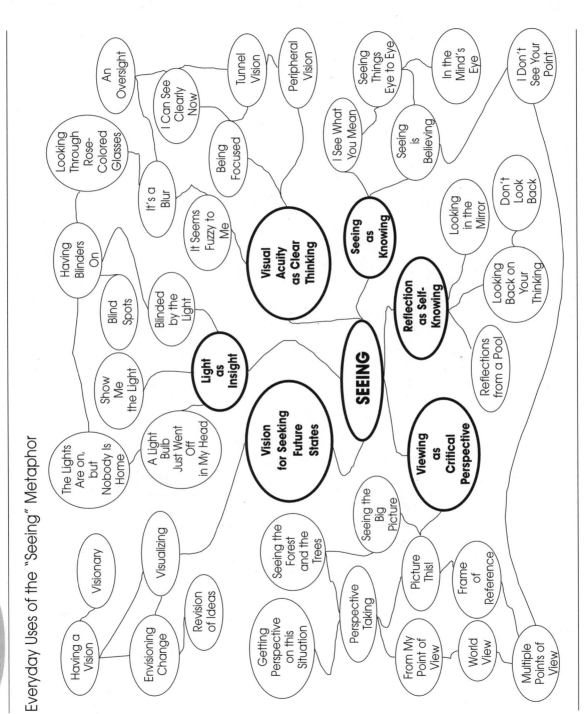

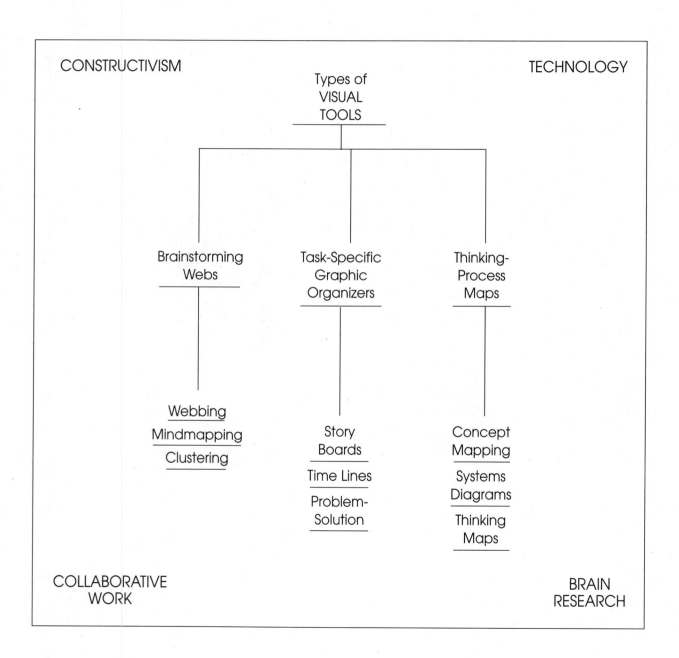

CONSTRUCTIVISM   TECHNOLOGY

Types of
VISUAL
TOOLS

Brainstorming   Task-Specific   Thinking-
Webs   Graphic   Process
                       Organizers   Maps

Webbing   Concept
Mindmapping   Story   Mapping
Clustering   Boards   Systems
                       Time Lines   Diagrams
                       Problem-   Thinking
                       Solution   Maps

COLLABORATIVE   BRAIN
WORK   RESEARCH

Introduction

It is today's students who will construct new knowledge. As we come more and more to believe that knowledge is not only interconnected but also interdependent, then we will see how much we need to provide students with dynamic new mental tools. These tools will help them unlearn and relearn what we have taught them so that they may build new theories of knowledge and also have the experience and capacity to create new tools for making their world.

(Hyerle, 1996, p. 127)

Lifespan Learning Tools

With these sentences I concluded *Visual Tools for Constructing Knowledge*, and with the same words I launch this *Field Guide*. As we enter a new century, it becomes ever more clear that visual tools—such as webs, organizers, and thinking-process maps—are practical, effective, dynamic, and learner centered. Importantly, these proven tools are theory-embedded, easily transferable across disciplines, and part of the assessment and self-assessment processes of learning.

Out of necessity, these "knowledge tools" are also desperately in demand. Teachers, parents, and employers face pressing questions: How are students dealing with the vast amounts of information they confront through endless media outlets? How are students working fluidly with the newest technologies to rapidly generate, change, and communicate information? The concern is real: few classroom tools exist to *explicitly* support learners in filtering, organizing, and systematically assessing raw slices of information. Reading comprehension, in the traditional sense of reading a text, is not enough: students must grapple with data in many forms delivered in high-speed chunks through numerous technologies. Few tools provide a concrete way to transform unprocessed information into useful patterns of knowledge, which are at once usable and easily communicated to others. And few tools, once mastered, can help learners manage the unknown overflow of information for a lifespan.

While visual tools have been shown to be effective in school, educators need to become aware that visual tools and software programs are now commonplace throughout the world of work. Graphical software tools for organizing information are now added to word processing and database spreadsheets to help workers and clients communicate smoothly as ideas, information, and inventories are moved through systems.

The question that drives the investigation of visual tools is this: How may we introduce students to and support their use of visual tools so that they can capably handle continuous change and become lifespan learners, as they progress from kindergarten throughout their senior years?

A second inspiration for this investigation has come from the intriguing conversations I've had with teachers about how these tools work for all students. Yet one of the most valued conversations came from a visit to a loan officer at my local bank. While my wife and I were reviewing documents for a loan application, he asked what I did for a living. I handed him *Visual Tools for Constructing Knowledge* as one artifact. He glanced through it, sat back, and chuckled.

By sheer coincidence, his wife, a high school mathematics teacher, had recently attended one of my workshops, and that morning she had been raving about how her students had been using visual tools. Nice feedback, I thought—maybe it will help with the loan! And there was more. The loan officer told us that he had already discussed with his wife how he was going to use several maps for his adult night course in banking procedures. The adult learners were having a hard time organizing, remembering, and linking together all of the concepts laid out in the course. What he had done in the past was just not working to engage students in the process of learning. Maybe using maps would work. At that moment I realized, again, that these are not merely tools for students to use today but in their future lives.

It also made me appreciate that every member of society is, by nature, a lifelong learner.

Back to the Future

In *Visual Tools for Constructing Knowledge*, I offered a more theoretical overview of the tools, broken into three basic and sometimes overlapping categories: brainstorming webs, task-specific graphic organizers, and thinking-process maps (see the figure at the beginning of the chapter). I explored these types of tools, highlighting that in practice they had some common visual *forms*, but significant differences in purpose and *function*. I also discussed three influences or frames of references for why visual tools are being used extensively in classrooms:

• The shift toward constructivism (and brain research) and the need for tools that support concept development and problem solving;

• Collaborative work involving generating, organizing, sharing, and evaluating *new* information; and

• New technologies that involve not only visual representations, but the "networking" of knowledge within *systems*.

These frames of reference are exactly what is required in today's workplace, and increasingly will be required in the future. Thus, students must reach another level of fluency with these knowledge tools to effectively and interactively use them with coworkers, with community members, and for personal problem solving for the rest of their lives. This need emphasizes one of the key themes of *Visual Tools for Constructing Knowledge:* Students must be the creative users of these tools, and we should not be duplicating blackline masters of graphics to be filled in like so many dittos. Blackline masters are just that: starting points that may become "masters" of us, that keep the mind thinking "in the box," as within the black lines.

Readers reacted to *Visual Tools for Constructing Knowledge* by saying they felt reassured that these are not just another strategy in a teacher's toolkit but, rather, devices that profoundly affect students' short-term work and long-term thinking abilities. The book also seemed to heighten educators' awareness that we have only begun to explore the implications and practical applications of various visual tools.

Why a *Field Guide*?

Though I am not a bird-watcher, I have always been fascinated by field guides that show pictures of birds, organized details, and an accessible display of information. Snippets of information are highlighted for quick reference and use. One can turn to any page in a field guide and dip into new information, so there is no need to read it in a linear fashion. I hope that this *Field Guide* is similar: the pages ahead are spiraling and recursive, going back into the first book and hooking onto key ideas, then propelling them into new applications and variations on models. While there is a logical order to the ideas, there is no need to read the book from front to back.

As you may have seen with a quick flip through the book, this *Field Guide* is not so much a guide to the theory of visual tools but a guide to what happens when using them *in the field*. Throughout this book you see an array of uses of visual tools drawn from early classroom years to workplace applications. The guide also includes

• Stories by educators, parents, and business people who summarize the use of these tools;

• "Overview" pages that give the theory, basic techniques, and novice-to-expert applications of key tools;

• Many examples of student and teacher work, software and book references, steps for implementation, tools for discrete learning tasks and for macro-problem solving;

• Quotes and quips and, I hope, tangents that will immediately take you to web sites and key resources.

The chapter sequence roughly parallels the chapters of the first *Visual Tools* so that the two can be easily used together.

The content within each chapter, however, is much different. Though the first few chapters offer a more theoretical picture—looking at lifelong learning and new insights into the brain, mind, and intelligences—many stories and applications go to the practical needs of classrooms. Chapters 3 through 5, respectively, focus on the three types of visual tools. Chapter 6 returns us to Thinking Maps®, a language of visual tools and software, and also takes us into the literacy landscape: reading comprehension. The final chapter, "Change Patterns," offers a view of visual tools as change tools, a fitting theme, as education, learning, and life itself are all processes of change.

Blind Insights

Occasionally we will also return to several key questions from the first book such as, Why are visual tools so effective—with so many squiggles, boxes, and feedback loops? One fundamental answer lies well below the visual representation systems of visual tools. I constantly return to the most memorable moment in my discoveries of visual patterns of thinking.

The moment I knew that visual tools were deeper than the facade of the boxes, ovals, and arrows that we have seen for years was at a follow-up visit to a school in Mission, Texas. I had been working with the school over time, using

Figure I.1

Flow of Chapters in *A Field Guide to Using Visual Tools*

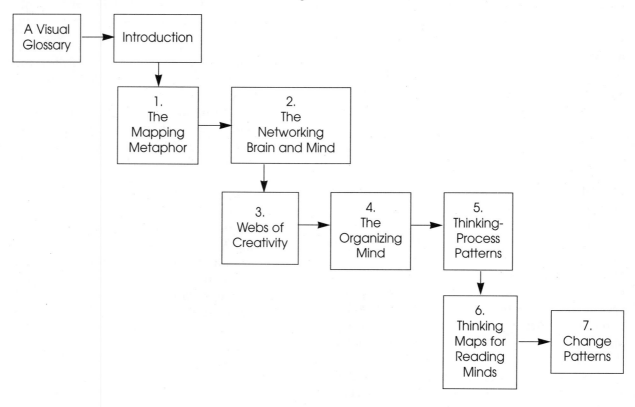

the language of Thinking Maps that I developed in 1988 as a foundation for thinking and learning. In a previous workshop at the school, a participant asked a question that stopped me cold like a deer frozen in the headlights. At first the question seemed to indicate a resistance to change, but then quickly turned to a deeper level: "These visual tools may work for most students . . . but not for *my* students. . . . you see, they are blind. How would you use visual tools with blind students?"

As quiet settled across the crowd (and wait time proved to be no great strategy at that moment), all I could offer were feeble mumblings about what an interesting question it was to think about.

When I returned a month later, with no answer in mind, the teacher who had asked the question handed me a videotape and several pale yellow, bumpy pages. And then I knew: her students were using a Braille machine to generate Thinking Maps on this special paper. We popped the video into the machine, and the whole faculty watched in awe. One of her students, particularly taken by "visual" tools, had created several Braille maps for generating context information about a writing topic using a Circle Map and then prioritizing the ideas into a Flow Map for sequencing. On the video this boy led his seeing peers in a discussion about the use of the maps and a reading of his description about a visit to a beach. The product was a beautifully descriptive piece of writing. The teacher was delighted with the outcome, and the student was improving. Of course, his "seeing" peers had been using the same array of visual tools: they could see the patterns . . . but he could *feel* them.

The moral I derive from this story is that most brainstorming webs, graphic organizers, and thinking-process maps are multidimensional, facilitating multiple intelligences: logical-mathematical, musical, visual-spatial, bodily-kinesthetic, linguistic, naturalist, and interpersonal and intrapersonal representations of the patterning and networking of information that is *already going on in the brain*. The brain, as an organism, has a specialized, continuously evolving, multidimensional, and dynamic *spatial* architecture. I have no better definition for high-quality visual tools as well: visual tools are conceptual architecture.

Now I believe even more strongly that visual tools provide one of the most direct routes for most learners—and maybe all but a few learners in our ever more inclusive classrooms—to show and communicate patterns of thinking. These tools leverage learning well beyond the common *linear* presentations of information that are but a shallow facade of the holism of human thinking and understanding.

Chapter 1 Overview

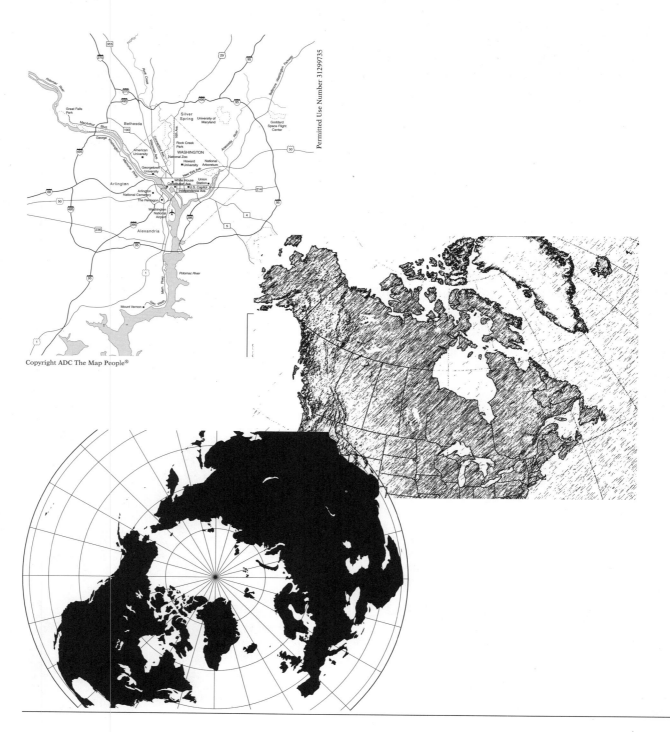

Permitted Use Number 31299735

The Mapping Metaphor

Map making has always been a central form of storing vital information about our surroundings and distant shores, from the ancient mappings of the earth and sky to solar systems. Humankind has always sought ways to discover and map new frontiers and find our way home by land and sea and, most recently, by air.

Cartography has been both a science and the gateway to new learning. The attempt to discover longitude in the 18th century was foremost in the minds of seafarers, traders, and governments, as latitude and longitude lines crossed and established the relationships between time and space that could guide adventurers and conquerors alike to unknown lands. The Lewis and Clarke expedition across the western region of North America, like any other journeys into new

> **Lewis studied maps in Jefferson's collection. He also conferred with Albert Gallatin, a serious map collector. . . . the problem was that west of the Mandans [an Indian tribe] nearly to the coast was _terra incognita._ And the best scientists in the world could not begin to fill in that map until someone had walked across the land. . . .**
>
> **(Ambrose, 1996, p. 80)**

landscapes, was an attempt to map territories unknown to a new republic so that commerce and land holdings could expand. The "map" that Lewis brought back to President Thomas Jefferson, of course, was technical in the geographic sense, commercial in the description of resources, and ethnographic in depicting cultures new to the adventurers. Now we send captainless ships to distant planets to map new territories off the curvature of the earth.

The "four corners" of our globe are now known, and our technical expertise has seemingly, and some say recklessly, hopscotched over our practical needs. We have access to electronically mapped terrain through GPS, or global positioning systems. We may be in our car with a map on a screen, guiding us around the corner or into another state. Likewise, and using similar technology for networking information, our children, gazing at a television or computer screen, access linked data from points around the world, and from different points of view. Those views may range from electronic explorers of knowledge on "the net" to mass marketers of goods to exploiters of graphic violence and other morally repugnant materials.

There are no new territories in the lower 48 states, as the greatest distance one can be from a road is only 28 miles. The new territories are of human imagination, interaction, communication. Why? Many are uneasy about students' capacity to access abundant information without necessarily having the tools or the time to organize, process, filter, and evaluate "info-glut" and "info-smog." The battles between schools and libraries and the ACLU are about the rights of a public institution to "filter" the Internet to prevent pornographic materials from getting into the hands of both child and adult.

The terms *network*, *world wide web*, *integrated*, and *Internet* are concrete expressions for what has become the central metaphor of this age: mapping. Mapping is both a metaphor for connecting and overlapping knowledge structures. As we see in this book, mapping is also the name for practical tools for mental fluency. Mapping is a rich synthesis of thinking processes, mental strategies, techniques, and knowledge that enables humans to investigate unknowns, show patterns of information, and then use the map to express, build, and assess new knowledge.

McKenzie (1998) talks about the potential of graphical organizers:

> As powerful electronic networks provide students with access to mountains of information, graphical organizers convert complex and messy information collections into meaningful displays.
>
> Graphical organizers have become an essential weapon in the struggle against info-glut and info-garbage.

They compress. They focus. They make interpretation, understanding and insight much easier.

Graphical organizers help students plan their research forays. They guide the gathering. They focus purpose. They show what is gained. They show what is still missing.

Graphical organizers sometimes serve as mind maps. They point to the destination. They identify related sites and sights. They help students to stay on track. (McKenzie, 1998).

> **The new information landscape is laced with potential for frustration and disappointment as well as opportunities, as the new abundance is often offset by disorganization. Equipped with the right tools and skill, fortunately, students can find meaning and develop insight despite the disorder. (McKenzie, 1998)**

This book is about the richness of the mapping metaphor for the 21st century, its central role in helping us understand how visual tools and technologies support learners in their human capacity to transform information into knowledge. We have the technical capacity to seek and show interdependencies: to network information on the world wide "web." So the "mapping" metaphor also opens up our central dilemma as we step into the new millennium: our students may have the technical link to information, yet few have the mental fluency to craft information into knowledge. This gulf between our students' technical expertise and the mental fluency is one of the barriers we must transcend to enact positive change in schools and the workplace. To be sure, we cannot go back to a time when information was so neatly packaged in books resting on library shelves.

Mapping in Everyday Life

So what does this map metaphor look like right now in day-to-day life in classrooms, in the workplace, and at home? How is the metaphor of mapping, the tools and techniques, embedded in what is now happening as lifespan learners discover the *terra incognita* of the modern landscape of knowledge? Here are some illustrations:

- After listening to a story, a reading group of kindergarten students excitedly offers new words to their teacher, who writes them in a mindmap.
- Each 2nd grade student sketches a long flowchart to sequence the plot of a short story, drawing pictures and writing words in each box. Their teacher collects and quickly assesses student work and adjusts instruction accordingly.
- A first aid book for parents contains 30 or more causal "if-then" diagrams describing responses to various symptoms exhibited by a child.
- Using two different cognitive maps, 4th graders generate a theme showing the hierarchical structure of the main idea and supporting ideas, which leads to a flowchart of logical steps to a persuasive writing prompt.
- Instructions for the family's new VCR include a flowchart of steps for programming favorite TV stations.
- Working in groups, 6th graders create various concept maps. They use software to map their understanding of the human body, compare their maps, and then present a synthesis of their knowledge of the software to their peers.
- A middle school teacher introduces an "escalator" conflict resolution graphic to help students see how conflicts escalate on the play-

ground, in their home life, and in examples from history.

- An advanced placement student uses a systems "feedback" cycle diagram to analyze the long-term, interdependent causes and effects of industrial pollution in the local wetlands.
- At the local university, a student uses concentric and overlapping circles to show the interactions among individuals and different social groups.
- At a local service station, a wall flowchart details the steps in getting service for your car.
- In a science lab down the street from the service station, a chemist maps out the interrelationships between a new drug and possible side effects.
- The president of a large multinational business distributes to employees around the world a "tree" graphic" showing the company's decision-making hierarchy (and chain of command). The company then uses mapping software for interactive conferencing.
- A microscopic pattern of circuits shows the interrelated dynamics of a new computer networking design.
- A consultant who works on the change process with businesses uses a mindmap to help middle managers think "outside of the box" about how to better communicate and lead in day-to-day operations.
- A college professor/educational writer/consultant works with school curriculum teams to "map the big picture" of the interrelated flow of content, skills, and interdisciplinary themes.
- A school administrator shows her board of directors a graphic synthesis of a "vision" for change developed from lists generated by working groups throughout the district.

As represented by these exemplars, the metaphor of mapping is grounded in the very same language of graphical representations of land, sea, and skies. Our daily language is now saturated with the idea of "mapping out strategies" and "networking" with information and people. Our most basic understandings in the scientific realm are based on mapping techniques spread across disciplines: we map the global weather patterns and the relatively unknown ocean floor; we map global transportation systems, computer chip circuitry, and telecommunication systems. Now we are mapping the human brain. All of the borrowed language of the mapping metaphor from cartography directly frames and names our discoveries in brain research. From the beginning, we have seen two *hemispheres* linked by a bridge, next *regions* of the brain, specific *locales*, and then the detailed system of neural networks. Figure 1.1 shows how even the understanding of brain functioning depends on visual mapping of the contours of activity. In this example, a special camera called a "magic eye" is used for scanning brain wave activity in different regions of the brain.

At this writing, we are on the edge of what many in the scientific field find as important as the race for the first landing on the moon: the "race" to map the human genome system. In a recent article about J. Craig Venter, one of the few leaders in this race, the "finish line" is described as

> a map of the entire human genome, the 80,000 genes that are thought to exist within our DNA. Altogether, this means finding more than three billion microscopic pieces of information—nucleotides, or bases, that are the molecular equivalent of letters—then putting them all in the right order and learning how to read them. (Belkin, 1998)

Venter is controversial from a scientific perspective not because he is attempting to identify every gene (as is the government-sponsored Human Genome Project). Rather, he is trying to extrapolate from a partial sequence of genes in a DNA string that the other genes exist in between—much like making a map of a city with

all the streets, but not filling in the details of each storefront. He is also in the center of a conflict from an ethical-commercial perspective: who will "own" this map, a so-called "Book of Life," the complete genetic code for humans? Figure 1.2 illustrates how a graphic representation is the most effective way to show this high level of complexity.

The Flow of Knowing

It is within this wider context that we will ask: Why is *mapping* and related terminology the *essential* guiding metaphor for our age? A short answer is that in this new century, the worlds of school, work, and work-at-home overlap to require a different set of tools—mental knowledge tools—beyond those for craftspeople and industry from generations gone by. In the workplace and in schools, the theories and realities of our knowledge and practical affairs are now slowly being translated into these new forms of tools, as highlighted in the vignettes listed earlier. We have not yet become fluent tool users in this new information age, as were hunters fluent with the bow, farmers with the plow, and line workers in shaping metal. We now shape information into knowledge as we once so fluently transformed a rocky field into furrowed crops and ore into folded metal. We now need to become fluent with tools for our thinking, *the transformation of information into knowledge.*

In *Flow*, Mihaly Csikszentmihalyi takes us back to another time when the daily job experience was more fluid: "Hunting, for instance, is a good example of 'work' that by its very nature had all the characteristics of flow. For hundreds of years chasing down game was the main productive activity in which humans were involved" (p. 152). Csikszentmahalyi guides us from hunting to farming to the crafts and cottage industries, including weaving—which were

FIGURE 1.1

Mapping Brain Activity

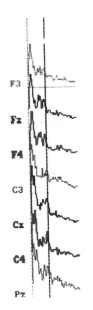

A brain map showing the frontal lobe activity while the student is working to see a three-dimensional image from a "magic eye" picture.

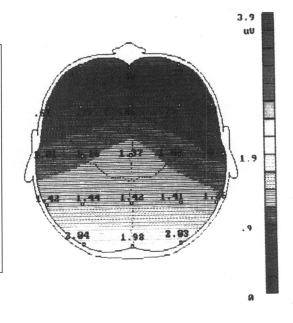

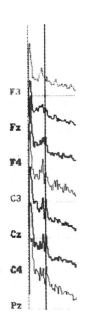

A brain map showing the change to the alpha brain activity when the student finally sees the three-dimensional image from a "magic eye" picture.

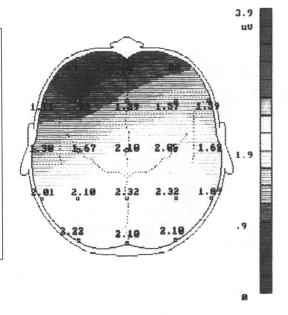

Source: Alcock, M. W. (1997, Spring). Are your students' brains comfortable in your classroom? *Ohio ASCD Journal 5*(2): 13.

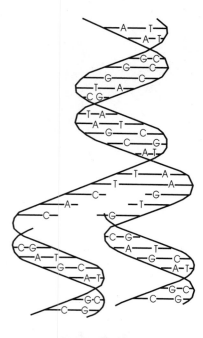

FIGURE 1.2

The Complexity of a DNA Strand

Source: Lowery, L. F. (1991). The biological basis for thinking. In A. L. Costa (Ed.), *Developing minds: A resource book for teaching thinking, Vol. 1* (rev. ed.) (p. 113). Alexandria, VA: Association for Supervision and Curriculum Development.

based in home "work"—through from the industrial to the postindustrial age, when

> such cozy arrangements conducive to flow were brutally disrupted by the invention of the first power looms, and the centralized factory system they spawned. . . . Families were broken up, workers had to leave their cottages, and move en masse into ugly and unwholesome plants, rigid schedules lasting from dawn to dusk were enforced. . . .
>
> Now we have entered a new post-industrial age, and work is said to be becoming benign again: the typical laborer now sits in front of a bank of dials, super-

vising a computer screen in a pleasant control room, while a band of savvy robots down the line do whatever "real work" needs to be done. (pp. 153–154)

As a post-industrial society, we have not yet adapted to "information" work, much as workers in the past century attempted to adapt to factory work. Much like the inadequate working conditions of early factories, our schools and workplaces are equipped with crude "information" tools.

Students are somehow expected to know more, learn more, do more, share more, collaborate more, create more, and to be more independent with information than ever before. Teachers, many of whom were trained long ago and find new technologies somewhat daunting, attempt to "work harder" with the same tools, and are not given the training required to "work smarter" with new tools.

Lauren's Map

The visual tools and technologies presented in this book are offered as examples of more polished "expert" information tools, not merely for low-level "processing" information like a computer, but for mental fluency, or the "flow of knowing."

One clear example of the capacity for mental fluency comes from my work with the students, teachers, and administrators at Friendship Valley in Carroll County, Maryland. For 18 months, the whole school faculty had focused on how to systematically introduce and use a toolkit of eight knowledge tools called Thinking Maps™ (see Chapter 6 for a full discussion of the eight Thinking Maps, p. 100). The central outcome for the training (every three months) was student-centered use of the tools: students were becoming fluent with the eight maps, using them in different contexts and according to their needs. They learned to see different patterns of content knowledge, filter out irrelevant information, assess their learning, and synthesize their ideas more fluently into final products such as writing. Here is part of the story from the whole cloth of this engaging school.

It is May 9, 1995, at Friendship Valley Elementary School in Carroll County. All the 4th graders are responding to the narrative writing prompt from the Maryland Performance Based Assessment. The school had been built five years before on the principles of Arthur Costa's "School as a Home for the Mind" and had strengthened its program over the years through a range of high-quality teaching and learning strategies.

If you had been in a certain hallway of Friendship Valley that morning—normally a stressful time for all participants in a school—you would have been startled by an ecstatic teacher running out of her room exclaiming, "They are using them on the test!" Many of her students, without coaching, were using various Thinking Maps to generate and organize information on the way to completing the prompt.

After collecting the testing documents, the teacher asked the students to write a statement about strategies they had used during the test. Many students, much like Lauren (not the student's actual name), responded with both a note and a representation of a Flow Map, one of the eight Thinking Maps. These students felt successful because they had become fluent with a practical tool that they had found to be usable in the moment. (Figure 1.3 shows Lauren's flow map and an explanation of her thinking.)

As it turned out, the final scores of Friendship Valley students were second across the state of Maryland on the combined scoring of the six performance assessments—including the writing—well beyond the mark where the school had previously performed.

By the time Lauren sat down for the writing test, she and her peers had become relatively flu-ent using Thinking Maps to detect and construct networks of knowledge on the way to final products. They had developed their capacities to be creative and flexible, to persevere and to be systematic. They had also developed a level of reflection and self-awareness of cognitive patterns that enabled them to go beyond the written form to visually unite map and mind, and to create a vision of what could be a final product.

Lifespan Learning in the Information Age

Many of us are uncomfortable with the stark, abstract, and somewhat numbing array of information made available to us on a daily basis. We seem a bit baffled by what to do with this information. Often it is not as neatly packaged as textbooks. Many of our students, seemingly undisturbed by the overflow of information, appear to revel in the novelty of bits of information flashing in front of their eyes and across their computer or television screens.

Yet the machines that our students and many parents use—information processors called computers—are a very limited extension of a slice of our human intelligences. We need tools that go well beyond the information crunching that computers provide: simply put, we need tools for thinking through problems that the computer cannot compute. Until we do this, we have not made the transition from information-glut into a healthy, flowing, information-rich working environment.

As a generalized statement, teachers and their students, managers and workers, do not have the tools to individually and collaboratively generate, organize, and evaluate information. We have old outline forms. We have a Venn diagram there, a flowchart here, a chart for organizing some information over there. But in many ways we have not become fully comfortable with

FIGURE 1.3

Lauren's Flow Map for Writing a Narrative

Testing

I used the flow map, and we have
been using them so much that when
I got done my first box I didn't
need to use it because the Flow map
was in my head. I got my topic
sentence down and my details just seemed
to flow right out.

the information age—we haven't learned new strategies for working with information—and many of us have become displaced workers and/or disoriented by new technologies.

Though we decry this situation, we have yet to identify and agree upon which skills and tools are needed as students evolve into adult workers. In an act of magical thinking, mostly we say that computers are the "information processing" tools. Wrong. Computers are a tool that needs to be programmed, and the information that comes out of the computer has to be "processed" by the learner.

A student may progress from daycare through five or six different schools to college and return for continuing education in later life. This same person can expect to hold six to eight different jobs in a lifetime (with a multitude of administrators or bosses). There is an undeniable need for people to have concrete, flexible, and transferable learning tools for self-assessment, information management (communication, organization, evaluation), and collaborative decision making.

From a purely economic perspective, towns, states, counties, and industries cannot afford to sponsor job training every time a worker changes jobs. We must also recognize that the quantity, quality, and representation of information has changed: we must go beyond linear representations of written text and find *mental* tools and technologies that are holistic, dynamic, learner-centered, and collaborative. Ultimately, these tools must facilitate lifelong habits of mind (Costa, 1996).

From Classrooms to Careers

If we look at a more finite perspective—what employers want from workers—we might start with the SCANS report, a document from the Labor Department of the Secretary's Commission on Achieving Necessary Skills (1991) under President George Bush. This report set the stage for ensuring that the world of work is addressed in the educational setting. The investigation led to a synthesis of workplace know-how and has helped propel the school-to-work, or school-to-career, movement in education. Much of this report is grounded in research showing that "more than half of our young people leave school without the knowledge or foundation to find and hold a good job" (1991, p. v.), that we are not developing the full academic abilities of most students, and that we are utterly failing the majority of poor, disadvantaged, and minority youngsters" (1991, p. vi).

The SCANS report identified three foundational pillars and five competency areas that should be the heart of instruction for students who will enter the work force (see Figure 1.4). Key to this report is that the foundations and competencies are brought to all students at all grade levels, rather than a framework for vocational education once students enter high school. Further, the recommendations seem to dovetail with many of the reform efforts identified by educators and descriptions of the characteristics of schools (see Figure 1.5).

What at first may look like a contradiction between the foundations—basic skills and thinking skills—in fact reflects where most teachers are focused. While the battle rages in the area of early reading comprehension, every other field is focusing on simultaneously building basic skills in the content areas and in higher-order thinking. The areas of thinking skills, student construction of knowledge, cooperative problem solving, problem-based learning, contextual learning, learner-centered focus, and the recognition that all students will improve their thinking are the keys.

The SCANS report, school-to-career programs, and reform efforts thus identify starting

FIGURE 1.4

SCANS Cause-Effect Thinking Map: What Employers Demand of Workers

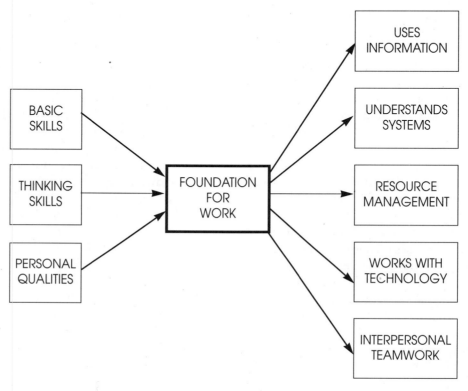

Source: Adapted from the Secretary's Commission on Achieving Necessary Skills (SCANS). (1991). *What Work Requires of Schools: A SCANS Report for America 2000.* Washington D.C.: U.S. Department of Labor.

and end points for workplace learning and life-long learning, but few efforts give us "the map" to guide us there. In the face of new technologies, information glut, and increasingly diverse populations, are we going to use the same tools we have always used in previous generations to support our current students?

One answer is all too clear as we see complex global issues soon overwhelming our own context: ominously, Albert Einstein stated, "The significant problems we face today cannot be solved at the same level of thinking we were at when we created them."

A Letter from a Parent

As we will investigate in this book, one array of tools that will help us meet the challenges of the information age—and is already being used in schools and much more in the workplace—is *visual tools*. These are the creative, dynamic, and

FIGURE 1.5

Characteristics of Today's and Tomorrow's Schools

SCHOOLS OF TODAY	SCHOOLS OF TOMORROW
STRATEGY	
• Focus on development of basic skills • Testing separate from teaching	• Focus on development of thinking skills • Assessment integral to teaching
LEARNING ENVIRONMENT	
• Recitation and recall from short-term memory • Students work as individuals • Hierarchically sequenced–basics before higher order	• Students actively construct knowledge for themselves • Cooperative problem solving • Skills learned in context of real problems
MANAGEMENT	
• Supervision by administration	• Learner centered, teacher directed
OUTCOME	
• Only some students learn to think	• All students learn to think

Source: Secretary's Commission on Achieving Necessary Skills (SCANS). (1991). *What Work Requires of Schools: A SCANS Report for America 2000* (p. 22). Washington D.C.: U.S. Department of Labor.

rigorous tools and linked technologies that may be used to activate, construct, and communicate knowledge seamlessly from kindergarten and beyond for lifelong learning. Let's look at an inspiring example of the dovetailing of these tools from school to the workplace.

In Wanganui, New Zealand, in the southern region of the northern island, is St. George's, a K–8 school that has implemented a visual tools approach over the past three years. All of the students, faculty, and administrators are fluent with these visual tools, and at workshops parents learn about graphic representations and how to support their children's use of them. There have been reports of parents using these tools after learning about them from their children (isn't that exciting?!). Headmaster Alan

Cooper asked parents to write about their perceptions of visual tools. Here are excerpts from parent Keith Smith's response:

I didn't know I was using anything with a name, like "Thinking Maps," until one day when Ben was doing his homework. I saw a kind of weird diagram and when I asked what it was, Ben said he was using a Thinking Map to plan a homework project. I noticed that he was doing a more developed version of how I often planned activities in my job at the time as national marketing manager for Suzuki motor vehicles.

I'd start with a topic or objective and take arrows out from below it in different directions, splitting the main subject into its key parts. Then I'd split each of these out over and over until I had every-

thing in my head about the job at hand on paper. Once done, I would cross out or edit items that were duplicated, irrelevant, or not a priority. . . . I'd then draw a neat, orderly copy for reference, and that would become my plan.

Now that I have seen some of what St. George's is doing, I have more consciousness of the possibilities and am increasing my use of the concept. Thinking back on how I started working this way (as it wasn't directly learned or taught), I think it evolved as the result of three sets of circumstances coming together:

1. Work pressures were dictating the need to simplify my working day, yet achieve better results.

2. I . . . tend to deal with several issues at once, jumping from one to the other as the subconscious throws up a thought in whatever order it chooses. . . . the Thinking Map allows me to jump around a subject effectively without losing the thread or an idea. I can scan the map and see the bigger picture and identify areas of insufficiency, etc. I find that sticking wholly to one train of thought and writing in depth about it . . . takes too long to prepare, and while it is often a good plan, it will invariably have a key area missed or inadequately covered. . . . the way I work now is . . . simpler, faster, and generates more effective planning. . . .

3. Suzuki (where I worked for 10 years) is a Japanese company, and the Japanese tend to use a lot of charts and diagrams, rather than extensive text, to communicate a concept. . . . I found myself adopting this approach more and more over the years and found that written (and verbal) communication approached in this way not only helped my dealings with Japan, but also benefited those with Kiwi's [an endearing term for New Zealanders].

I ended up writing things (such as dealer bulletins) more simply and clearly. [M]y last year at Suzuki, I prepared an annual advertising and promotion plan, involving an expenditure of almost 3 million dollars, which was accepted by top management here and overseas, delivered the result planned, and consisted of only two sheets of paper. Previous thinking would have generated a 15-page epistle, which no one (including myself) would have referred to again. . . .

I presented a sales training speech a few weeks ago [at my current job] and made my handouts in a kind of Thinking Map format, as I had limited preparation time and felt people would relate to them easily. They were fast and easy to prepare, didn't require fancy treatment (color or computer graphics), and did the job well. The feedback I got was very positive.

. . . I see it [the Thinking Maps concept] as a way of simplifying certain tasks while simultaneously multiplying effectiveness. I guess the more clarity we can generate, then the less content is required.

For me, the Thinking Maps concept goes hand in hand with the next step: implementation. Tasks planned utilizing Thinking Maps and then implemented to continue the concept have great potential to work successfully. Actions have more chance of being carried out logically and with purpose, backed up with good explanation, etc. Communications are more likely to be presented in a way compatible with how we think, feel, talk, and see. A bit like how a photograph tells a thousand words.

Theory into Practical Tools

This parent's letter reveals that behind the day-to-day interactions, communications, problem solving, and decision making, visual tools can provide the practical tools for thinking. Though surfacing slowly and without fanfare, dynamic graphic representations have become practical classroom tools and keys for success for students from kindergarten to college, and for those who go immediately into the workplace. As we see in this letter, these tools work for all ages.

Ultimately, though, these are not isolated strategies for specific content tasks, but tools for constructing mental models within a new constellation of theories based on present scientific understandings of living systems. As we turn to the next chapter for a deeper look into why these tools fit our needs at this moment in history, we will find that in the post-Newtonian age, we are moving away from thinking about the world as made up of fragmented "things," linear "one-to-one" causes, and mechanistic, static structures. Rather, we are coming to understand the world in terms of interdependent webs of relationships, patterns in process, and dynamic systems.

> New theories penetrate into the world of practical affairs when they are translated into methods and tools . . . . "Tool" comes from a prehistoric Germanic word for "to make, to prepare, or to do." It still carries that meaning: tools are what you make, prepare, or do with. (Senge et al., 1994, p. 29)

Visual tools with names such as webs, organizers, and maps are now used in the classroom and workplace for putting these evolving theories into practice. And most of all, these tools are preparing learners as they enter into and influence another critical transition for human culture: moving from conveyor-belt thinking to developing reflective habits of mind for lifespan learning.

Schemas
Mind

Habits of
Mind

Multiple
Intelligences

Brain
Patterning

Systems
Thinking

Natural
Networks

The Networking
Brain and Mind

Whenever we look at life, we look at networks.

—Capra (1996, p. 82)

Teachers around the world are often mystified by the mismatch between their perceptions of students' thinking and classroom performance. You may have heard yourself say:

• "I know that he has great ideas, but he can't seem to get them out in his writing! His writing is always a jumble."

• "She has amazingly creative ideas, but has a very hard time articulating them."

• "I give my students the information, but when they come back with it—if they can remember it—it's a disorganized mess! They simply don't know how to organize their ideas."

• "I tell them the steps, but they often have to be told over and over again to get it right."

These very same concerns may be heard in the workplace as well, as supervisors recognize the talents in people yet are perplexed by the quality of work produced.

> **Seeing with Both Eyes**
>
> I look at a person with two eyes. One eye tells me what he is; the other tells me what he can become. (Horton, 1990, pp. 131–132)

In this chapter we will look at how visual tools facilitate learners' capacities to move fluently from internal brain and mind functions to the products of their thinking. How can we see with one eye how they are thinking while keeping in mind what they can become? This is a metaphor used by Myles Horton (1990), adult educator, literacy teacher, and founder of the legendary Highlander Folk School in Tennessee:

I like to think that I have two eyes that I don't have to use the same way. When I do educational work with a group of people, I try to see with one eye where those people are as they perceive themselves to be. . . . I try to find out where they are, and if I can get hold of that with one eye, that's where I start. You have to start where people are, because their growth is going to be from there, not from some abstraction or where you are or someone else is.

Now my other eye is not such a problem, because I already have in mind a philosophy of where I'd like to see people moving. It's not a clear blueprint for the future but movement toward goals they don't conceive of at that time.

I don't separate these two ways of looking. I look at people with two eyes simultaneously all the time, and as they develop and grow, I still look at them that way, because I've got to remind myself constantly that they're not all they can be. (Horton, 1990, pp. 131–132)

We will look through multiple windows to see how visual tools facilitate the dynamic, evolving, lifelong development of brain, mind, and intelligences through the following:

• A 21st century definition living systems offered by Fritjof Capra,

• A structure of the brain as found in recent research,

• Habits of mind as offered by Arthur Costa, and

• A multiplicity of intelligences identified by Howard Gardner and Daniel Goleman.

Setting the stage, let's first look at a practical example in the context of the classroom. Examining some action research conducted by Bob Fardy—a K–5 Science Curriculum Specialist with the Concord Public Schools in Concord, Massachusetts—will enable us to investigate the more theoretical issues of natural and neural networks, habits of mind, and multiple intelligences.

Bob uses two eyes in the way Myles Horton conveys the idea of an educator: one for seeing where students are and another for moving them to another level of understanding. In the next section we will see expressed in his writing and maps how Bob and his students use visual tools to seek basic information, create an assessment rubric for their own learning, and thus provide lifelong tools for transforming informa-

tion into knowledge. We can also see how this process of using visual tools provides learning tools that students may take beyond the classroom and into their careers.

Bob's experience is thus the fulcrum between the last chapter—focusing on school to work—and this chapter, which takes us into brain, mind, and intelligences. As you read Bob's description, consider how students, with facilitation, are building knowledge from the ground up, from bits of concrete information they are discovering to the creation of basic abstract, conceptual patterns, to a wider mental model of something that is common to every elementary school education: rocks.

Addressing Two Questions with Many Stones

BY BOB FARDY

One of the exciting challenges I face as a curriculum support person is the multidimensional nature of my job. As a curriculum specialist, I design and develop science units and provide support to classroom teachers during program implementation. My responsibilities also involve staff development, working with teachers as they examine and explore a range of pedagogical issues about teaching, learning, and assessment.

During the 1997–98 school year I developed an introductory rocks and minerals unit, which I subsequently taught as a series of inquiry-based lessons in 11 2nd grade classrooms. During this time, "wearing my staff development hat," I worked with the 2nd grade teachers on science assessment. Together we explored the use of open-ended questions as a tool for assessing student learning and examined the role of graphic organizers and visual tools in the assessment process. In December 1997, the teachers participated in a districtwide staff development workshop that fo-

cused on the use of visual tools. This helped frame my conversation with the 2nd grade teachers and set the stage for our work for the next few months.

While working with 2nd graders as they studied rocks and minerals, and dialoguing with their teachers about visual tools and assessment, I decided to link these two initiatives. The convergence of the curriculum initiative (the rocks and minerals unit) and the staff development initiative (the visual tools/assessment discussions) provided the teachers with the opportunity to see—through a content-specific lens—the versatility and effectiveness of visual tools. Using the rocks and minerals unit as a vehicle for exploring visual tools, I began to reflect on my work with the teachers and their students. This crystallization of my thinking led in turn to two compelling questions:

1. In what ways do visual tools facilitate student learning?

2. How do visual tools enhance and extend the classroom teacher's repertoire of assessment skills and strategies?

Using the term "killing two birds with one stone" to refer to this convergence may seem a bit dissonant for a curriculum specialist who conducts nature walks and other environmental science activities for children. To rephrase the expression, I discovered that indeed I was addressing two questions with many stones.

At the beginning of the rocks and minerals unit, I introduced the students to three visual tools from the Thinking Maps® model (see Chapter 6, p. 100): the Circle, Bubble, and Double Bubble Maps. In our school district, classroom teachers often use the K-W-L strategy (Ogle, 1988/1989) when their students begin a new topic or unit of study. The strategy is an effective way for students, at the beginning of the unit or lesson, to identify what they already know (K), what they want (W) to know about a topic, and what they

have learned (L) at the conclusion. As both teachers and students were familiar with this approach I introduced the students to the Circle Map and asked them to share what they already knew about rocks.

The Circle Map proved to be an effective brainstorming tool for the students. In each of the 11 2nd grade classrooms I recorded and displayed the students' responses between the concentric circles of the map. This tool helped me to carefully avoid any kind of linear listing, clustering, or linking of their responses that might imply or infer some kind of hierarchical ordering of their ideas and/or making connections between and among their comments. In this way the Circle Map served as a classroom mirror, reflecting the fluency and flexibility of students' thinking, ideas and information at that moment in time. Later, at the appropriate time, the Circle Map became a springboard from which the students would organize their ideas using clustering or webbing techniques.

After many years of teaching, I am continually amazed at the depth and breadth of information and the highly sophisticated level of thinking that young children bring to a learning situation. As the students continued to brainstorm what they knew about rocks, I began to see the Circle Map as more than a mirror that reflected the students' responses. The map was also serving as a window, providing a means to access and assess the students' thinking. I could identify their prior knowledge and surface some possible misconceptions and alternative conceptual frameworks. Indeed, the Circle Map was emerging as an effective tool for both assessment and brainstorming.

This visual tool clearly invited and encouraged the students to continually add more ideas and information. After several minutes I asked the students how they might organize and cluster their responses. We noted that there were several statements that dealt with "Uses of Rocks," while other responses could be placed into categories

FIGURE 2.1

What Do You Know About Rocks? A Circle Map of Students' Responses

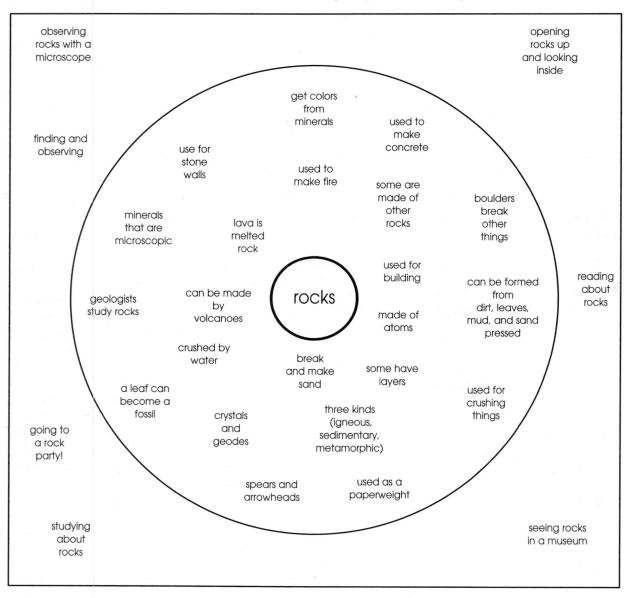

such as "How Rocks Form" (Processes), "Properties of Rocks," and so forth.

For me the distinguishing feature of the eight Thinking Maps, as compared with more traditional visual tools, is the frame of reference, which, as a metacognitive device, added another dimension to the lesson. As the students, classroom teachers, and I reviewed the Circle Map, we acknowledged the fact that "we already knew many things about rocks." Transferring our attention to the frame of reference, I asked the students, "How did you learn what you already know?" In responding to this question, the students were reflecting on their own learning and at the same time were informing me about the diversity of learning experiences that had been their avenues for acquiring knowledge and constructing meaning. The students identified their "ways of knowing and learning" in the outside frame of their Circle Map (see Figure 2.1).

Having surfaced and assessed the students' prior knowledge, I distributed rock samples (granite) to each student and introduced another Thinking Map, the Bubble Map. With the aid of hand lenses, the students examined the samples of granite using multi-sensory observations. Then, using the Bubble Map, they recorded their descriptions of the properties of granite. After a few minutes the students shared their map (see Figure 2.2).

Most important, as they shared their maps, the 2nd graders identified the discrete types of properties that they had been observing: color, texture, shape, patterns, luster, minerals in the rock (composition), size, and smell. We called the generated list of rock properties our "rock rubric," and my students subsequently referred to it as they observed more rock samples (gneiss) and recorded their observations using a new Bubble Map.

Having shared their Bubble Maps about granite with their classmates and using the rock rubric as a guide, the students made and recorded even more observations about the gneiss samples. As the students increased the number of observations they began to expand their map, adding more "bubbles" of properties as needed. Now the students were beginning to take greater ownership of the visual tool, adapting it to meet their needs. Rather than a static "fill-in-the-bubbles worksheet," the Bubble Map became a dynamic, versatile, open-ended graphic with a certain "elasticity" that could be stretched in tandem with their thinking.

In the concluding moments of this lesson I asked the students, "How are granite and gneiss alike and different?" Each student literally had both samples in hand in order to compare and contrast these two types of rocks, but to facilitate our discussion the students also had two Bubble Maps, which could be merged into a third Thinking Map, a Double Bubble Map (see Figure 2.3).

In science, students are constantly comparing and contrasting objects, organisms, phenomena, events, and ideas within and about the natural world. It has been my experience that we as teachers often use Venn diagrams as "the" graphic organizer for compare-contrast. However, I have observed that often certain graphic organizers—such as Venn diagrams—can be problematic. Children, particularly young children, as concrete learners can at times become focused on the seemingly fixed format and nature of the graphic. For example, if the Venn diagram is drawn with a relatively narrow area of intersection, does that imply that there is a limited commonality between the objects being compared? If I had asked the students to compare granite and gneiss by constructing and using a Venn diagram, how would they determine to what extent to overlap the circles?

The Double Bubble Map clearly was a more user-friendly tool for the students to manipulate as they compared granite with gneiss, developing naturally from the separate Bubble Maps they had created and more in keeping with a constructivist approach to learning.

FIGURE 2.2

A Bubble Map by Students Shows Attributes of Granite

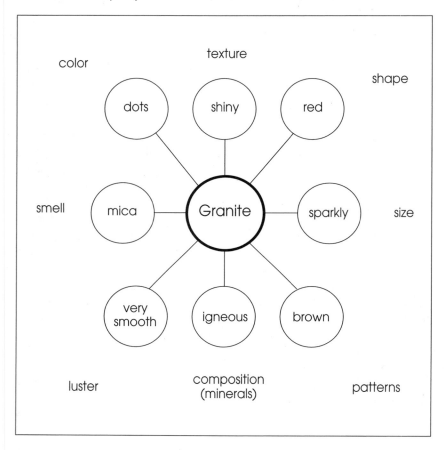

Following this first lesson with rocks and minerals, the students had additional opportunities to observe and describe the properties of 10 other types of rocks including conglomerate, sandstone, pumice, obsidian, slate, shale, limestone, marble, basalt, and granite schist. These additional rock explorations set the stage for the second lesson (a week later), when the students sorted and classified the 12 kinds of rocks according to their own classification systems. I introduced a fourth Thinking Map, [the Tree Map, Tree Map illustration] which supported students with another key scientific process, categorization, or the creation of taxonomies.

As I reflect on my efforts to "address two questions with many stones," I find that the insights gained and discoveries made about the relationship between visual tools and teaching, learning, and assessment to be both rewarding and challenging. In the true spirit of science, in searching

FIGURE 2.3

A Double Bubble Map by Students Compares Granite and Gneiss

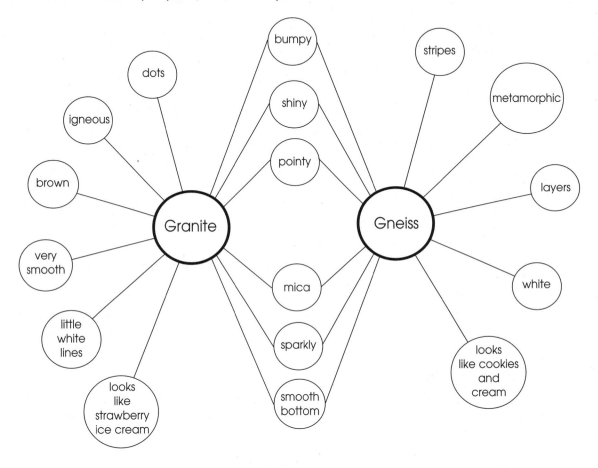

for answers to my questions, I have in turn generated more questions:

• How could I have integrated the other four Thinking Maps—the Brace, Flow, Multi-Flow, and the Bridge Map—into the rocks and minerals unit?

• Are certain visual tools more developmentally appropriate for students of different ages?

• Are certain visual tools appropriate to specific content?

• How will I build upon this work next year with grade 2 teachers and students?

• How will I expand my efforts to include other grade levels and science units?

The answers to my initial two questions have become newly formed stones that when cast into the *water create a rippling effect of new and emerging questions to be explored with students and teachers next year.*

Networking Nature, Brain, Mind, and Intelligences

If we look closely at the above rock rubric activities and then allow ourselves deeper reflection on the use of visual tools, it becomes apparent that students are seeking patterns in nature. Their brains are actively detecting patterns, and through a range of habits of mind and their multiplicity of "intelligences," they are organizing the raw data into schemata and graphically surfacing these relationships. They are inductively generating new mental models of the dynamic interconnection of information into knowledge, or concepts.

How does this happen? We begin by looking at the natural world, then the human brain, the mind and its habits, and finally frames of mind, or what we call "intelligences."

Nature Exists as Patterns

It may be that visual tools have evolved at this time in history as tools for learning directly out of the need to cope with a fundamental shift in our understanding of life systems. In times gone by we were plenty satisfied by text or oral language.

If the existing paradigm is based on a dynamic systems view, rather than a mechanistic view of life, then tools that help us *map* these networks become paramount. Of course, our perceptions of the natural world also influence our present conceptions of the human brain as well.

Over the past 50 years there has been a dramatic shift in the scientific and philosophical underpinnings of our understandings of life forms. In *The Web of Life* (1996) Fritjof Capra

brings together quantum physics, information theory, systems thinking, and theories linking the brain, mind, and cognition into a view of life. Here is a condensed view of Capra's definition of a living system:

> a living system has a pattern of organization that is physically structured and activated by a life process that embodies these. (Capra, 1996, p. 161)

The key characteristic of this definition of a living system is the *pattern of organization* of an organism. Capra states:

> In the study of structure we measure and weigh things. Patterns, however, cannot be measured or weighed; they must be mapped. To understand a pattern we must map a configuration of relationships. (1996, p. 81)

This underlying principle is what is now guiding brain researchers and educational leaders at this time in our history to use tools and techniques that support students in seeking, constructing, and, ultimately, understanding the *patterns* of knowledge that ground every discipline we teach, and that support connecting every discipline together.

For example, in the rock rubric, Bob Fardy and his students revealed that they were not measuring rocks but beginning to create *networks* of information from their observations. They were mapping the configuration of prior knowledge, identifying their frames of reference, describing and then more discretely comparing different rock forms, and finally creating an abstract taxonomy of the information. While certain measurements could be taken later, these investigators were uncovering patterns of information, not measuring the qualities of each isolated specimen.

Of course, one of the barriers to studying rocks is that students—even with a field trip—

> **Maps are frames of reference. In them, a student must find a way to relate new information to other information. . . . teachers often have not been exposed to creative map-teaching models or forfeit map learning to accommodate the mandate for higher test scores.**
>
> **(Caine & Caine, 1994, p. 46)**

would have a hard time fully studying rocks in context. Bob did the next best thing by having hands-on specimens. What was lost was a systems analysis of the samples in context.

Importantly, one of Bob's emerging questions had to do with the other possible maps that could be used. As we shall see in Chapters 5 and 6, the study of systems is richly facilitated by using cause-effect and systems diagrams to model how different rocks were formed over time.

The Brain Is a Pattern Detector

If we believe nature exists as patterns, then it is no wonder that the experts in brain-based learning all agree on one thing: the brain makes sense of the world by *constructing* patterns from the world. The focus on "patterning" is thus the entry point to understanding the connection between brain functioning and visual tools:

> The overwhelming need of learners is for meaningfulness. . . . We do not come to understand a subject or master a skill by sticking bits of information to each other. Understanding a subject results from perceiving relationships. The brain is designed as a pattern detector. Our function as edu-

cators is to provide students with the sorts of experiences that enable them to perceive "the patterns that connect." (Caine and Caine, 1994)

Indeed, that we must *perceive* this pattern to understand it is a convincing clue for looking for new visual learning tools. We must now find ways of showing relationships, patterns, networks, and systems, because, as Capra states, there is no way to measure patterns. . . . we must map patterns. The idea that patterns of organization of an organism are the fundamental starting point for life leads us to the basic brain research that now excites and informs so many educators, parents, and even politicians.

The array of linked patterns in the brain is *always* more complex than the linear form in which we normally communicate these ideas in classrooms. As Bob Fardy pointed out from his experiences with the rock rubric, too often students are giving us merely linear lists of information without having to organize the information into patterns.

Unlike the repetitive listing of information so often found in textbooks and in classrooms, the brain is unconsciously reconstructing bits, shreds, and strands of related information from all over its physical frame while integrating sensory inputs into a multitude of overlapping patterns. As educators, we know that students have much more going on "in there" than we "get out" of them. Why? Many say that the brain is being underutilized. Less obvious is the case that what is actually "going on in there" has few pathways of "getting out of there" other than on the lined paper of schooled, linear representations. The brain's structural capacity for constructing patterns and the mind's cognitive processing capacity for expressing complex interrelationships in networks of knowledge is being dramatically under-represented in linear strings of words, numbers, and other traditional symbol systems.

> **Visual tools are effective as learning aids. I want to find out what others have learned and how they connect it to prior learning. One end-of-course strategy is to cover a wall with flip chart or butcher paper. Then let small teams design a huge visual representation of what was learned. Either they can cooperate to create a synergistic visual map, or they can split up the content and each team makes their material as part of the whole. When it's done, it's a mural that creates common, unifying thinking—and it opens up new possibilities where gaps exist or connections are open.**
>
> **(Jensen, 1998a)**

For example, when we ask students essential and complex, higher-order questions, we are activating an unbelievable network of linear and holistic firings of neural networks. But then we ask them to answer in linear terms: verbally, in writing, or by strings of numbers on the page. They respond by looking dumbfounded. Could it be that they do not have the tools to think and express their ideas holistically? Or is it that their rapidly patterned ideas are being condensed into short answers and exclusively in linear terms? The true mismatch is between the brain's capacity to pattern and the weak set of tools we provide to students so that they can fully represent their thinking.

The mismatch is apparent because of the structure of the brain. Remarkably, unbelievably, the brain as a structure is capable of absorbing 36,000 visual images in every hour. How can this imponderable information be true? It is because the sophisticated visual capacity of our brain system is beyond the conscious processing of our mind: research approximates that between 80 and 90 percent of the information received by the brain is through visual means. Though our auditory and kinesthetic modes of "sensing" are complex, the *dominant* mode through which our brains most efficiently filter most information is through our eyes. The human brain has evolved to become positively *imbalanced* toward being primarily a visual imager/processor. As Sylwester (1995) describes:

> The site of 70 percent of our body's sensory receptors, our eyes begin the cognitive process of transforming reflected light into a mental image of the objects that reflected the light. Light rays (photons) enter an eye through the system of the cornea, iris, and lens, which focuses the image on the thin retina sheet at the rear of the eyeball. The rays are absorbed by the retina's 120 million rods and 7 million cones, with each rod or cone focusing on a small, specific segment of the visual field. . . .

Though most any memory is constructed from activations all over the brain and all modalities must be reinforced, the brain has been evolving over time toward visual dominance. Even if we each believe that we are strongly "kinesthetic" or "auditory" or "visual," consider that each of us is still taking in more information "visually" than through other modalities. We need to understand, and thus teach and learn with, this imbalanced strength in mind: most of our students and most of us as we read this page, are strong visual learners.

Current brain research has provided many insights into how the brain unconsciously takes

> . . . The one million fibers in the optic nerve of each eye carry a summary of the vast amount of data that the [retina's] 127 million rods and cones receive.
>
> . . . Further processing (forward in the cortex) combines line segments into shapes, colors them, combines them, locates them in space, names them, and contemplates their meanings. At this point, sensory processes are being transformed into thought processes.
>
> (Sylwester, 1995, pp. 61–62)

The Mind Organizes into Schematic Patterns

The tantalizing details of recent brain research provide support for decades of cognitive science research drawn from behavioral studies focused on the mind at work. The dovetailing of brain and cognitive science research is grist for many more books, but one of the most important links is between the networking structure of the brain and the "schematic" processing of the mind.

Schema theory—which was long ago overshadowed by brain research—brings the net-

in and consciously processes information. Pat Wolfe represents three major stages of information processing within the dynamic system of the brain: paying attention, building meaning, and extending meaning (Wolfe, 1991). Most visual tools provide flexible cognitive patterns to students and teachers that are congruent with and facilitate each of these stages.

These findings all give background as to why graphics are now becoming essential classroom tools. In *Visual Tools for Constructing Knowledge*, I review three related types of tools: brainstorming webs, graphic task-specific organizers, and thinking-process maps. Each of these kinds of tools, and in different ways, concretely supports patterning and networking of information, organizing information into knowledge from various sources, seeking meaning within prior knowledge, and linking of isolated bits to holistic, interrelated systems.

> The impact of visualization on memory and recall has been demonstrated in numerous studies. In one, subjects were shown as many as 10,000 pictures, and then later shown some of these same pictures along with other pictures they had not seen. Under these conditions, they were able to recognize more than 90 percent of the pictures they had already seen [Standing, 1973].
>
> It appears that not only are visual tools extremely effective in assisting students to initially process and make sense out of abstract information, they are also taking advantage of our brain's almost unlimited capacity for images. (Wolfe & Sorgen, 1998)

working structure of the brain and the schema-generating mind together. The physical structure and actions of the brain are networking information, physically chunking and storing bits of information in certain regions. When these are "called up" from all over the brain, these isolated bits are integrated together.

On a micro level, this integration supports the moment to moment, instinctual, unconscious, and repetitive processes of life. On a macro level, when larger chunks are "called up" to a more conscious level, the process of building or constructing of cognitive structures from experience occurs. Schemas are not necessarily patterns that are conscious to the human mind, but are the building blocks of cognition and mental models. As Daniel Goleman points out, schemas are the transitional, ghost-like forms that carry raw experience to an organizational level:

> The packets that organize information and make sense of experience are "schemas," the building blocks of cognition. Schemas embody the rules and categories that order raw experience into coherent meaning. All knowledge and experience is packaged in schemas. Schemas are the ghost in the machine, the intelligence that guides information as it flows through the mind. (Goleman, 1985, p. 75)

Goleman links brain research with cognitive science and the early beginnings of Emotional Intelligence in the book *Vital Lies, Simple Truths: The Psychology of Self-Deception* (1985). Here he shows the connection between brain research on attention and research on schemas:

> Schemas and attention interact in an intricate dance. Active attention arouses rele-

> Mind is not a thing but a process—the process of cognition, which is identified with the process of life. The brain is a specific structure through which this process operates. The relationship between mind and brain, therefore, is one between process and structure.
> (Capra, 1996, p. 175)

vant schemas; schemas in turn guide the focus of attention. The vast repertoire of schemas lies dormant in memory, quiescent until activated by attention. Once active, they determine what aspects of the situation attention will track. . . . they also determine what we do not notice. It is here where the structure of brain and the processes of mind unite: the neural networking as a growing structure and the mindful attention and/or inattention to the organization of experiences. (pp. 79–89)

Because schemas are often but not exclusively networks of grouping and categories of information, visual tools complement the structure patterning of neural networks and schematic structures of concepts. Piaget and many others since confer great importance on the capacity of a learner to assimilate and accommodate new information and concepts into a prior held schema. Then the schema, and the physical structure of the brain shifts and reforms into a new structure.

If schemas are the bridge between the structure of the brain and the processing mind, visual tools may be a bridge between the patterning mind and a outward representation of these patterns.

Habits of Mind as Patterns of Behavior

So how do we understand and respond "intelligently" to the patterns that are before us? How do our habits of mind attend to all of these patterns that the brain has detected and the mind has organized?

Capra and many critics of Western philosophy and education point out that traditional paradigm for studying living systems has been based primarily on the study of structures. Therefore, so has our educational system. Translated into classroom life, students have more often been asked "What are the parts?" rather than "How do all of these parts interactively work together in a system?" We are beginning to shift from asking students to regurgitate discrete parts of topics, toward a different way of perceiving the world—one requiring that they show *how* these discrete parts integrate into dynamic patterns. The idea of seeing the interconnective nature of things in the world is not a new thought, as revealed by the da Vinci principles (Buzan, 1996) shown in the box on this page.

Thus, educators are now shifting toward more process questions and with this shift from the study of structures to an integrated study of patterns and processes, we will also change or add to our basic tools for understanding, constructing, and communicating knowledge. In a sense, we are in a transitional time of habituating our students to thinking in patterns.

How our minds respond to stimuli is bound up by the storehouse of overlapping, interconnected schema, yet we are not passive minds and we make decisions—often unconsciously about how we respond. These decisions are guided by general habits of mind initially researched by Reuven Feuerstein, as fully described by Art Costa. Consider these behaviors and habits of mind:

- Are we *impulsive* when confronted with an overload of information?
- Are we *empathic* when listening to another point of view?
- Are we *flexible* when we are in unfamiliar contexts?

> **Leonardo da Vinci's Principles for the Development of a Complete Mind**
>
> 1. Study the science of art.
> 2. Study the art of science.
> 3. Develop your senses—especially learn how to see.
> 4. Realize that everything connects to everything else.
>
> (in Buzan, 1996, p. 26)

- Are we *systematic* when working through a problem?

These habits of mind may be barriers to learning or powerful facilitators of knowing. In the "rock rubric" lessons, students were staying on task and actively using visual tools to remain flexible and systematic in their exploration. They also used tools to help them listen and learn from one another as they actively put their minds together with the maps.

These habits of mind and others are often facilitated when visual tools are in practice. It is also clear that different types of visual tools—with varying purposes and outcomes—actively facilitate different habits of mind. Just as a carpenter or chef has particular tools for distinct outcomes, so too does each type of visual tool seem to support certain clusters of habits of mind, or intelligent behaviors (see Figure 2.4).

Within each of the next four chapters we will look closely at how the 12 habits of mind shown in this figure seem to cluster around webs, organizers, and thinking-process maps.

FIGURE 2.4

Habits of Mind: A Triple Web of Behaviors

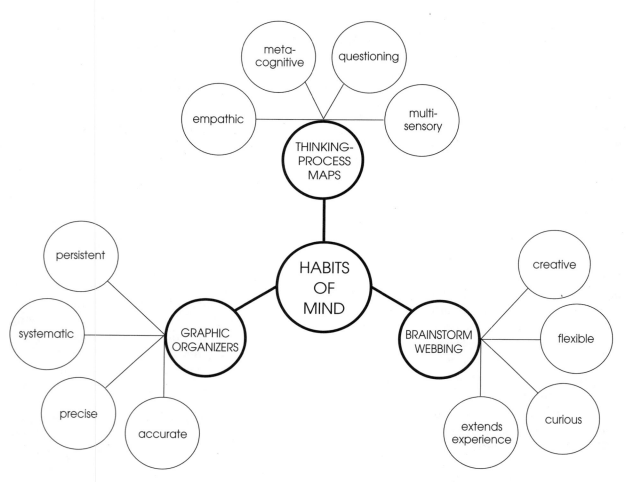

Source: Hyerle, D. (1999a). *Visual tools and technologies* [Video]. Lyme, NH: Designs for Thinking.

Multiple Intelligences as Active Patterns

If we look at the brain as a pattern detector and habits of mind as defined by Costa, we can begin to see that the intelligences described by Howard Gardner are really about how the multiplicity of patterns are expressed—or represented in different ways. The eight intelligences (and possibly a ninth) are more easily understood as ways of representing knowledge. In Gardner's fascinating book on cognitive science, *The Mind's New Science*, he brings forth the idea that this new science traffics in representations:

the cognitive scientist rests his discipline on the assumption that, for scientific purposes, human cognitive activity must be described in terms of symbols, schemas, images, ideas, and other forms of mental representations. (Gardner, 1985, p. 39)

Symbols and symbol systems thus are the translators or medium of the brain/mind/body connection into the realm of intrapersonal and interpersonal communications. What Gardner has done is asked us as an educational community—and as a larger community encompassing work, family and personal leisure time—to expand our awareness and appreciation of different representation systems. The full expression is in products of mind:

> Symbols and symbol systems gain their greatest utility as they enter into the fashioning of full-fledged symbolic products: stories and sonnets, plays and poetry, mathematical proofs and problem solutions, rituals and reviews. (p. 301)

We can here make some simplistic correlations between some of the eight intelligences (representation systems) and visual tools: linguistic, logical-mathematical, visual-spatial, interpersonal and intrapersonal intelligences are directly supported by brainstorming webs, graphic organizers, and thinking-process maps. These visual symbols support the construction of networks of language and logical processing, and are based on a spatial patterning of information. These tools also provide a way of communicating frames of mind, perspectives, and mental models among people, as these tools have been used in schools and work for facilitating change in mind-sets. And these maps become a mirror of the mind at work, thus facilitating an internal dialogue and self-assessment.

Yet there is something deeper at hand with visual tools than surface-level links to various intelligences: the brain and mind is a structure-process organism that detects and constructs patterns, and visual tools are foundational for sensing, thinking, and feeling across all of these intelligences. As basic patterning tools, visual tools support learners as they seek patterns across all symbolic systems, as these symbolic systems are bound up in schemas. As Daniel Goleman (1985) points out,

> Schemas are intelligence in action. They guide the analysis of sensory input. . . . Schemas determine which focus attention seeks, and hence what will enter awareness. When driven by emotions like anxiety, schemas impose themselves with special force. (pp. 82–83)

Given these overlapping views, I am suggesting that what integrates and also makes distinct different intelligences is the brain mind schemas, or webs of relationships, patterns, and interdependence.

In Joseph Novak's new book about concept mapping™, *Learning, Creating, and Using Knowledge*, he quotes his co-researcher David Ausubel:

> If I had to reduce all of educational psychology to just one principle, I would say this: The most important single factor influencing learning is what the learner already knows. Ascertain this and teach him accordingly. (1998, p. 71)

Ausubel was writing some 30 years ago, in a time when teacher-centered learning was locked into place and when adults still remained in a job for a lifetime, before we shifted toward cooperative learning, collaborative problem solving, and dynamic information technologies. He would now add, I am sure, that we must find ways to have *the learner become aware of his or her own patterns of knowledge and habits of mind*.

As we shall see in the remainder of this book, a rich array of visual tools provides a way for students to discover what they know as they creatively weave strands of information into meaningful knowledge.

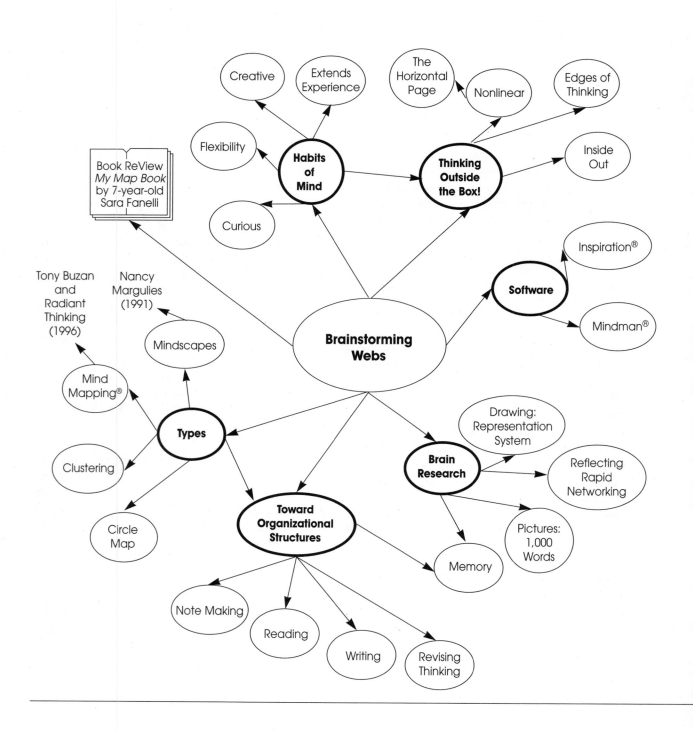

Creative

Extends Experience

The Horizontal Page

Nonlinear

Edges of Thinking

Flexibility

Habits of Mind

Thinking Outside the Box!

Inside Out

Book ReView
My Map Book
by 7-year-old
Sara Fanelli

Curious

Inspiration®

Tony Buzan and Radiant Thinking (1996)

Nancy Margulies (1991)

Software

Mindman®

Mindscapes

Brainstorming Webs

Mind Mapping®

Drawing: Representation System

Types

Brain Research

Reflecting Rapid Networking

Clustering

Pictures: 1,000 Words

Circle Map

Toward Organizational Structures

Memory

Note Making

Reading

Writing

Revising Thinking

3

Webs of Creativity

Drawing Out Student Thinking

Highly developed cave drawings have existed since the beginning of humankind. Now, as a literate culture with written language, we are slowly coming back to drawings as an essential way for learners to show their thinking and to build mental models. Brainstorming webs of many kinds derive from a synthesis of drawing and language. Of the range of techniques that I will share in this chapter, most include the use of sketches, drawings, icons, graphic figures (ovals, boxes, linking lines)—all integrated with key words.

An example of this range of forms is found in a children's book, drawn by a child. In *My Map Book* (Fanelli, 1995), 7-year-old Sara Fanelli draws almost every kind of map that is presented in this chapter and in this book. In this richly colored book, the fascinating view of the world by a 7-year-old emerges, all hand drawn and painted. She includes traditional maps of everyday places in her life, such as her bedroom, a roadway, the playground, the village, and a nearby seaside. She

also maps the physical parts of objects in her life: her own face, her dog, including "dog dreams." She even includes a map of her own tummy, and if you have never seen the world from the point of view of a belly button, find this book!

Sara also draws out more conceptual mappings, such as an interconnected family tree, a flow of a typical day, a network of favorite colors and linked information ("Why do I like the color red? Cherries!"). A precious map that will tug at your heart strings and make you think about the capacity of children to express emotional understandings is a map of Sara's heart. Finally, this hardbound book cover opens up to become a poster, a larger "synthesis" map of many of the pieces from various maps in the book. On the back of the poster is an open area guiding readers to create their own map.

Importantly, there are no page numbers on the 28 large pages. This is no ordinary, linear book. It is an insightful way into the nonlinear maps of Sara's mind. This kind of a book could be made by anyone of any age. It provides an array of pictures of the world views, a brainstormed web of correspondences and connections. Most important, it opens the mind to a creative web of perceptions that may be looked back on for review and reflection.

The Brain and Brainstorming

Brainstorming webs are *natural bridges* between and among brain functioning, radiant capacities of our thinking, habits of mind, and the typical linear form of representing knowledge in classrooms. The associative power of the human brain is facilitated through and ignited by a high degree of open-ended brain networking. It is understandable and somewhat haunting that many "webs" look similar to the newest pictures we have of neural networks, neurons being the building blocks of the brain that communicate with one another. Axons send information to other neurons; dendrites (Greek for "tree") branch out with the cell body to receive information—networking neuron to neuron at a rate of 10 million billion transmissions per second. Figure 3.1 shows the complex, tree-like branching forms created by neural networks.

> **Radiant Thinking (from "to radiate," meaning "to spread or move in directions, or from a given centre")** refers to associative thought processes that proceed from or connect to a central point. The other meanings of "radiant" are also relevant: "shining brightly," "the look of bright eyes beaming with joy and hope" and "the focal point of a meteoric shower"— similar to the "burst of thought."
>
> (Buzan, 1996, p. 15)

Brainstorming webs are mostly open systems for thinking "outside of the box." This means that the students creating webs often share no formal or common representation system. Often private graphic languages develop in classrooms, each related to the personality of the thinker. But to believe that brainstorming webs should not or cannot evolve into more formal, holistic structures is to deny the great depth of these visual tools. Clustering, Mind Mapping®, and Mindscaping, as we see in this chapter, are all forms that the developers of these tools see as a process of moving from generation to organization to transformation of ideas and concepts. With advanced development of a graphic, these visual representations may also be final products for presentation in a classroom or boardroom.

A mistaken belief of many educators is that brainstorming webs are a first step rather than an enduring process that continues and that even extends beyond a final product. I have even heard from teachers that students may brainstorm information and then not even refer to the document during the later processes of completing a project. Often, then, brainstorming webs are perceived as a static visual picture—the snapshot of creative energy—that is somewhat disconnected to further creative and analytical work, rather than a running video of evolving mental models.

This premature halting of the brain in an open state happens by moving too quickly away from the brainstorm before deeper processing and revision of the web occurs. Students may grow a web outward while never seeking the interdependencies that lay at deeper reaches in their neural networks.

Mental Fluency

Drawing is the key to webs of creativity, and once this door is opened, mental fluency is facilitated. Lana Israel, a self-described "13-year-old

FIGURE 3.1

Schematic Side View of Cortex Shows Tree-Like Branching of Neural Networks

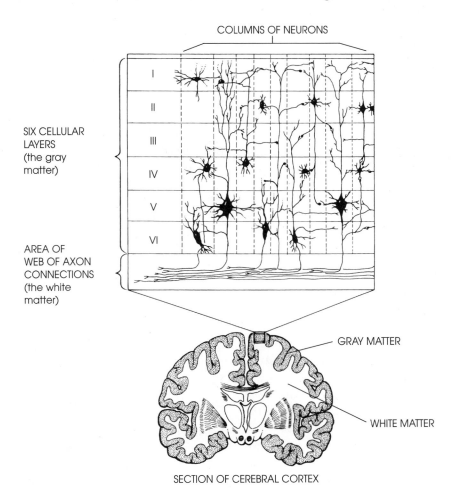

COLUMNS OF NEURONS

I

II

SIX CELLULAR
LAYERS
(the gray
matter)

III

IV

V

VI

AREA OF
WEB OF AXON
CONNECTIONS
(the white
matter)

GRAY MATTER

WHITE MATTER

SECTION OF CEREBRAL CORTEX

Illustration by Lydia Kibiuk.

Source: Sylwester, R. (1995). *A Celebration of Neurons: An Educator's Guide to the Human Brain* (p. 46). Alexandria, VA: Association for Supervision and Curriculum Development.

kid living in Miami, Florida," conducted a two-part experiment that became the central thread of her book on Mind Mapping, *Brain Power for Kids* (Israel, 1991). As a school science project investigating Mind Mapping and links to the brain, Lana asked her peers to write a draft of a speech on the topic "My Ideal Day." Later, after introducing Tony Buzan's Mind Mapping® to these students, she asked them to do the same exercise with specific Mind Mapping techniques.

Here are some of the responses from the two events:

Statements After Writing a Draft:
- I was more concerned about spelling than my ideas.
- I could not write fast enough.
- I was unable to go back and add ideas or expand.
- I was worried about neatness.

Statements After Mapping a Draft:
- My ideas flowed faster, and I felt more creative.
- I could see connections between ideas easily.
- I could always build up all ideas.
- I got an amazing amount down.

It is clear even from this informal experiment that writing often gets in the way of the natural networking-capacity of the brain to think, create, and even construct logical connections.

Of course, this concept also applies to speaking. How many times have you, your colleagues, and your students been unable to clearly articulate your ideas when asked a question? Often we are scrambling to make a linear response without thinking and being able to express a rich answer to the question. So here is a radical proposition that most educators, parents, and office managers might bristle at upon first consideration: speaking and writing *often* get in the way of our most creative and analytical thinking. Because of the mental frames that often constrain classroom contexts—time, neatness, precision, and a narrow focus on the final product—we don't ask students for their "messy" and generative thinking. Rather, we get them immediately on the relatively rigid track to linear outputs: speaking and writing.

Creative thinking time, or unfettered "think time," is given the short end of the stick in classrooms, other than in specific activities that are deemed "creative" such as "creative writing." There has been much discussion about the research on "wait time" (Rowe, 1974) so that we provide even just a few more seconds of time for students to respond to our questions. Yet we give students very little extended "wait time" for sketching out their "thinking." We want them to produce (and most of the products are linear) while not investing in creating (and most creative thinking is nonlinear).

Mental fluency is the capacity to comfortably, without fear and with ease, make associations with an openness of mind, without blinders or preconceived notions about the ultimate product of the thinking. As we have learned from recent brain research, emotion is the first filter—and possible shut-down mechanism—for us as we respond to the environment (Goleman, 1995). Students need to feel that their thinking can be safely opened, exposed. Students thus need extensive experiences in being able to think fluently, so that when they are asked to respond verbally or in writing, they have developed automaticity in thinking. This capacity is in every child, and with the visual-information age upon us, the capacity to effortlessly develop ideas and network information through visual representations is *essential*.

Thinking in Pictures

An extreme case of the power of mental fluency and visual thinking is expressed in a unique book, *Thinking in Pictures*, by Temple Grandin (1996). Temple Grandin has a Ph.D. in animal science, and has created numerous unique and highly successful inventions for use in the cattle industry. Temple is also severely autistic. She has, as she described, a remarkable capacity to form a virtual visual library in her mind:

> I store information in my head as if it were on a CD-ROM disc. When I recall something I have learned, I replay the video in my imagination. The videos in my memory are always specific. . . . I can run these images over and over and study them to solve design problems. . . . each video memory triggers another in this associative fashion, and my daydreams may wander far from the design problem. . . . this process of association is a good example of how my mind can wander off the subject. (Grandin, 1996, pp. 24–25)

While this is an extraordinary example—certainly outside the scope of a typical student—this individual's experience gives us insight into

---

Think of your eyes as the projector lens, and your visual cortex as the screen that registers the rapid sequence of sunlight-to-starlight still pictures it has received from your retina—still pictures that it translates into a continuous mental motion picture that functions magnificently beyond mere flickering shadows on the wall at the back of a cave. (Sylwester, 1995, p. 62)

---

basic human capacities. The use of extraordinary examples is actually a foundation in the process of discovery whereby Howard Gardner developed his theory of multiple intelligences. He looked at the far reaches of human capacities and extrapolated from these cases to reveal these capacities within all of us.

In the case of visual association, retention, and generation of ideas, we know as practitioners that many if not most of our students are strong visual learners. As mentioned in Chapter 2, brain researchers believe that between 80 and 90 percent of the information received by the brain is visual. Temple's rich descriptions of her thinking processes are a magnification of what most of our students are able to do, given the practice and tools to do so. Yet most students after kindergarten are given a vertical lined page for their thinking. It's important that we also give them a horizontal, blank page for developing pictures of their thinking (see Figure 3.2).

Webs for Facilitating Habits of Mind

During the short amount of time it takes for students to become comfortable and then fluent with brainstorming webs, or Tony Buzan's more specific techniques of Mind Mapping, it becomes clear that a cluster of habits of minds (Costa, 1996) centered on creative thinking are actively engaged and facilitated. While educators have found it easy to identify verbal and written fluency as key objectives, we have not been activating mental fluency, which matches the holistic networking capacity of the human brain.

Art Costa refers to this process of mental fluency with such words as ingenuity, originality, and insightfulness. By continuously probing and adding ideas via branching techniques, we can use all of the different types of brainstorming webs as tools for seeking the edge of our thinking, and thinking beyond the edge. In the world of business this has been called "thinking outside the box." This process also opens up other habits of mind that Costa identifies: flexible thinking, curiosity about problem solving in general and

Experiment! A Picture of One's Thinking

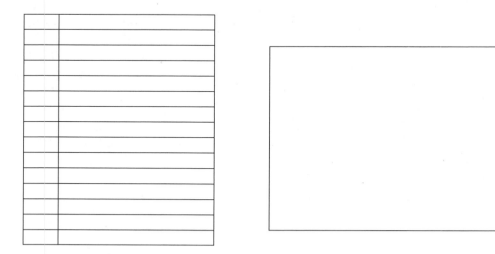

Before you ask students to take notes on a chapter, write a draft of a story, or do a prewriting activity, ask them to take out a blank piece of paper and place it horizontally before them. Ask them to draw their thinking by first sketching a picture or using words in the center of the page. They may sketch a picture, use words, or just doodle. As they proceed through the chapter, or collection of information, ask them to continually add to the picture. After the session is over, tell them to scan their page. Then ask them to close their eyes. Ask: *How many of you can see your drawing as a picture in your mind?* You will be surprised, and your students will be on their way to using webs in a more systematic way in your classroom.

one's unique patterns of generation of ideas (see Figure 3.3).

Becoming flexible and curious through visual branching and linking ideas also interacts with the habit we wish to develop in students: their capacity to transfer experiences between and among personal, work-related, and academic learning contexts. Webbing supports students in stretching their thinking outside of the standardized frames of mind that usually constrain thinking to the immediate context of learning. Each of these habits of mind—flexibility, curiosity, and transferring of experiences— are key habits for developing the more general

quality of creative thinking. All of the types of brainstorming webs shown here center on open-mindedness while also providing a "safety net" for seeing how generative ideas link together to form more coherent pictures of thinking and feeling.

An excellent starting point for developing mental fluency in visual form is to use very simple "clustering" techniques with students and adults of all ages. Figure 3.4 describes clustering and provides a rubric for using the technique. As the figure shows, this form requires no special drawing ability, nor is there a focus on more advanced Mind Mapping techniques.

FIGURE 3.3

Bubble Map of Four Habits of Mind

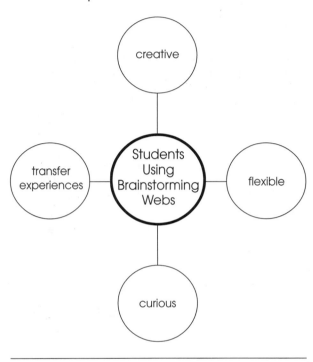

and irrelevant expressions and concepts before focusing on the evolving piece of work. Then comes the process of discarding the unusable drafts, brush strokes, doodles, and shards that are absolutely necessary for the creative process, but not for the final product.

Fluency with Information Overload Using Visual Tools Software

In times gone by we have promoted mental fluency and the facilitation of habits of mind within the framework of spoken language and written text. No more. We must now also open this frame to see that fluency of mind is essential within the environment and influence of a range of new technologies *and* access to an infinitely growing supply of unfiltered information. As students become learners in the world of work, they will be required to weave information together from different sources as they work at a computer station, laptop, palm computer, or with projection units in front of working groups.

Interestingly, one of the greatest needs we now all recognize—for students being able to filter vast amounts of information from the Internet—is partially answered by emerging software programs based on webbing and other types of visual tools. An extremely flexible software program for creating graphic representations is Inspiration®. I reviewed this software in *Visual Tools for Constructing Knowledge*, so I'll add only cursory comments here.

Importantly, a first cluster may evolve into a graphic that is overburdened with information. When a cluster becomes unmanageable with too much information and too many links, ask learners to revise it into a more organized web by pruning bits of information, much as the brain naturally prunes away unused information. As the learner focuses on later stages of the process—on the way to a final product—he or she may need to delete or reform whole portions of the cluster that have become irrelevant. It is important, however, for learners not to discard the various revisions, as they become a cumulative assessment of the emerging ideas.

These techniques resonate with most artists, as artists must generate excessive, redundant,

Many of the webs and organizers created for this book were created with Inspiration or Thinking Maps software programs. (See discussion of Thinking Maps software, Chapter 6.) Inspiration Software, Inc., has upgraded its earlier versions and has also published several resources for users, such as *Classroom Ideas Using Inspiration®* (1998). In these resources, classroom teachers

FIGURE 3.4

Clustering Overview

BACKGROUND: The "clustering" of ideas using simple ovals and words was first highlighted for educational use by Gabriel Rico. She established a strong link between associative thinking, creativity, drawing, and fluency of thinking and emphasized clustering as a prewriting strategy. The simplicity of the techniques for clustering enables all learners to begin the process of being in touch with their own holistic flow of ideas. Rico suggests that after creating initial "clusters" students revise their drawings into more focused "webs," thus leading to greater clarity of thinking and writing.

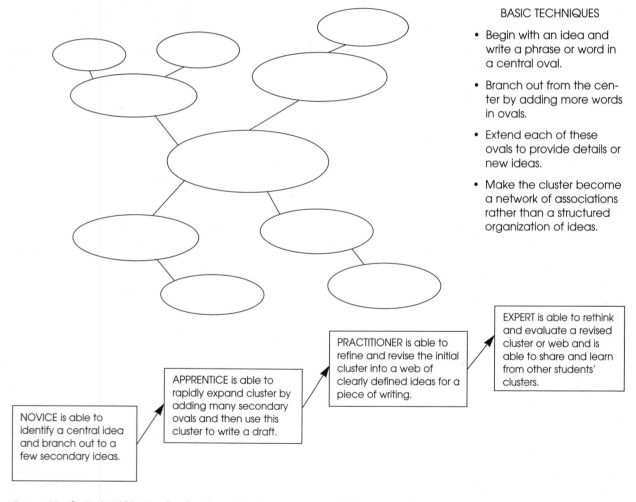

BASIC TECHNIQUES

• Begin with an idea and write a phrase or word in a central oval.

• Branch out from the center by adding more words in ovals.

• Extend each of these ovals to provide details or new ideas.

• Make the cluster become a network of associations rather than a structured organization of ideas.

NOVICE is able to identify a central idea and branch out to a few secondary ideas.

APPRENTICE is able to rapidly expand cluster by adding many secondary ovals and then use this cluster to write a draft.

PRACTITIONER is able to refine and revise the initial cluster into a web of clearly defined ideas for a piece of writing.

EXPERT is able to rethink and evaluate a revised cluster or web and is able to share and learn from other students' clusters.

have written sample lessons integrating this software, other technologies, and reading selections.

The example provided here shows that the teacher brings Inspiration into the flow of an interactive classroom. Students are working together and independently with a CD-ROM for accessing information, Inspiration software for analyzing and synthesizing the information, and a word processing program for writing reports. Figure 3.5 shows the lesson Marjorie Adamczyk, an intermediate teacher at Altamonte Elementary School in Altamonte, Florida, created and an example created by her students. While the lesson plan in Figure 3.5 is "technology heavy," it illustrates what the world of work actually requires. Workers regularly research information sources such as CD-ROMs. They must then synthesize the information and deliver it in written form to others in the working group or to administrators.

With Inspiration Software, students and teachers have a user-friendly visual-technology tool for providing the bridge between raw data (preprocessed information) and a unique document. They can return to their web and add information, include immediately available clip art, move it around, color it in a rainbow of organizational areas, or delete it. They may also press a key and the whole web transforms into a traditional outline form. All of these functions provide students with the capacity to move from initial vision, to revision, to final concepts. This process is demonstrated quite well by David Schumaker, former teacher, principal, and director of the State of California Central Coast Consortium Professional Development Division in the following description.

Idea Mapping

BY DAVID SCHUMAKER

My father once told me that while he was working at General Electric in Schenectady, a memo was circulated asking for people to think of a new way to "dehydrate bread." From that question came the idea for the GE Toaster Oven, one of GE's best-selling appliances. He went on to explain that if the question had been, "How can we build a better toaster," the image of a square box with slots in the top would have clouded people's thinking and the idea for the toaster oven may never have come.

When I am looking for input on an idea or to understand a process, I like to start with a very primitive diagram of my thinking. I do not want to "poison the well" with too much stuff so that I can get other people's thinking instead of mine. I usually start with my Inspiration program and map out a few points to illustrate my question and, then, with copies in hand, ask people I respect to go to lunch or meet for breakfast. During the meeting I give them a copy of the graphic, and we discuss the question and I take notes on my copy of the diagram.

In one example [Figures 3.6, 3.7, and 3.8 show three versions of the idea map as it evolved] *the questions I asked were "How does the concept of student outcomes fit into the restructuring of schools? How do we decide what the outcomes should be and determine student progress toward meeting them?"*

After one or two meetings, I go back to my computer and "flesh" out my diagram with ideas gained from the meetings. After doing some further research, I then print out a new diagram. I send this to the people who had input into the process for feedback. I also ask others to meet with me to give input on the more detailed idea. Finally, after several stages I produce the complete map and then use it in my writing or decision making.

Fluency with Inspiration, as with webbing itself, is remarkably quick. Of course, this fluency, at the click of a button, does not replace the power and personal touch of hand-drawn webs. It simply provides another avenue for expressing holistic understanding of mental mod-

FIGURE 3.5

Webbing and Writing with Inspiration Software

Created by: Marjorie Adamczyk, intermediate teacher
Altamonte Elementary School, Altamonte, Florida

Grade Level: 3–5

Subject: Social Studies, Science and Language Arts

Overview

After extensive exploration of a CD-ROM called "Inventor's Lab," published by Houghton Mifflin, during which students take a virtual reality field trip around three inventors' labs, students use Inspiration to create a web as notes on what they learned. From the web, students write a report.

Skills

1. Exploring technology
2. Organizing ideas
3. Cooperative learning

Materials needed

1. "Inventor's Lab" CD-ROM by Houghton Mifflin
2. Inspiration K–12 Education Edition software
3. Word processor

Preparation

1. Before beginning webbing, conduct the following activities. For each activity, students should work in groups of 2 or 3.
   a. For about 40 minutes each day for a week, students explore the CD-ROM "Inventor's Lab." They take a virtual reality field trip into one of the three inventors' labs, where they manipulate and test items in the lab. They read about the social and political concerns of the time and read about and create a time line of the inventor's life.
   b. For about 40 minutes each day for two days, students use time line software (or Inspiration) to create a time line from information they gathered from the CD.

Activity

1. For about 40 minutes each day for two days, students use Inspiration to create a web and an outline that shows what they learned from the CD.

Example of James Watt Web

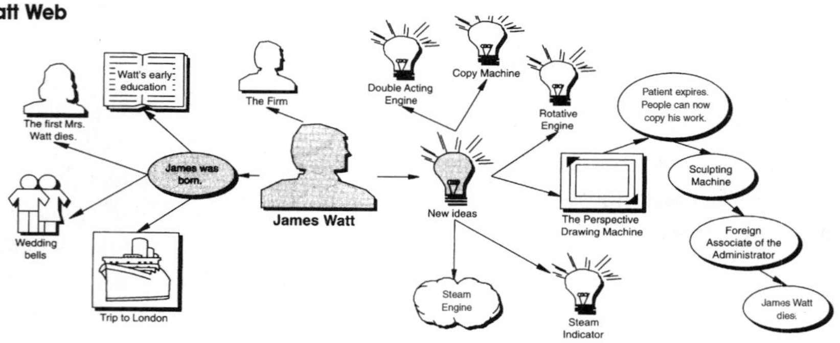

Follow-up activities

1. Using the web and time line as notes, each student (working alone, not in groups) writes a report. No other notes are allowed. Students can either use the web as a rough outline for their report or switch the web to an outline and work from there.
2. The report must cover three times in the inventor's life: his early years, the years he produced inventions, and later years. It must also include how his inventions affect us today.

Source: Inspiration Software, Inc. (1998). *Classroom ideas using inspiration®* (pp. 25–26). Portland, OR: Inspiration Software, Inc. E-mail: www.inspiration.com. Phone: 503-297-3004. Copyright © 1998 by Inspiration Software, Inc. Reprinted with permission.

FIGURE 3.6

Student Outcomes Idea Map: Version 1

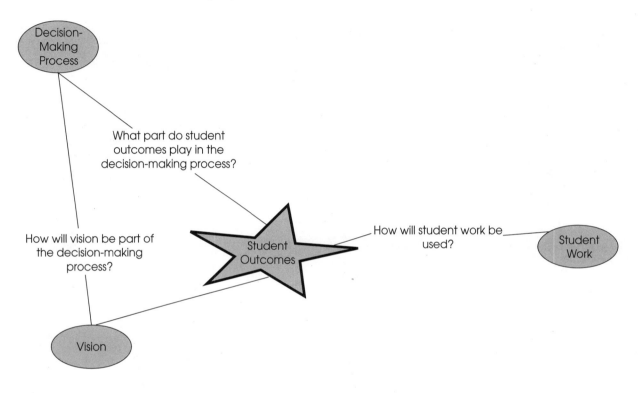

els, models networking constantly in the human mind. David Schumaker's example is well taken: the software may be used as layers of new information are learned and integrated into a changing structure.

Mind Mapping

Brainstorming webs come in infinite arrays, though most learners start in the center of a blank page, as we have seen above with "clustering," and then branch out according to the idiosyncratic designs created as an idea expands. This idea came from the revolutionary work of Tony Buzan decades ago (Buzan, 1979) and is captured with new vigor and depth in what may be considered his culminating text, *The Mind Map Book*.

A Mind Map always radiates from a central image. Every word and image becomes in itself a subcentre of association, the whole proceeding in a potentially infinite chain of branching patterns away from or toward the common center. Although the Mind Map is drawn on a two-dimensional page it

FIGURE 3.7

Student Outcomes Idea Map: Version 2

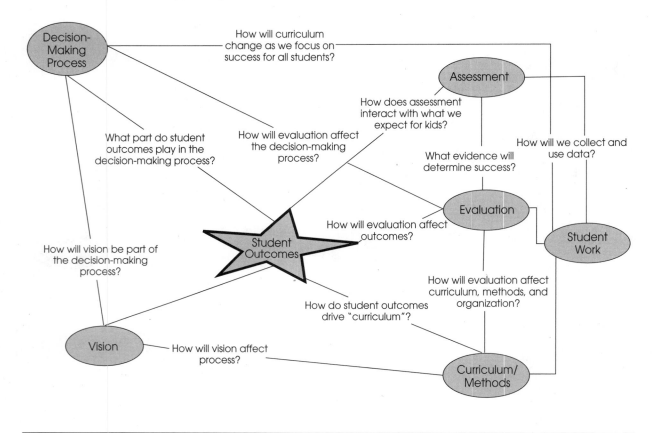

represents a multi-dimensional reality, encompassing space, time, and color. (Buzan, 1996, p. 57)

The open form and purpose of brainstorming webs preceding from a key concept in the center promote creative generation of ideas without blinders. The basic techniques of Mind Mapping (see Figure 3.9) evolve to reveal personal styles, especially with the addition of colors, drawings, depth, and multi-dimensions.

While most educators think of Mind Mapping as focused on the "generative" beginning point for entering a new subject, even greater implications for learning exist when students use Mind Mapping over time to concretely "draw" from their past knowledge everything they know about a topic and then link newly accessed information to their Mind Map. Drawing on past knowledge is a habit of mind essential for transfer of information and skills to new con-

Student Outcomes Idea Map: Version 3

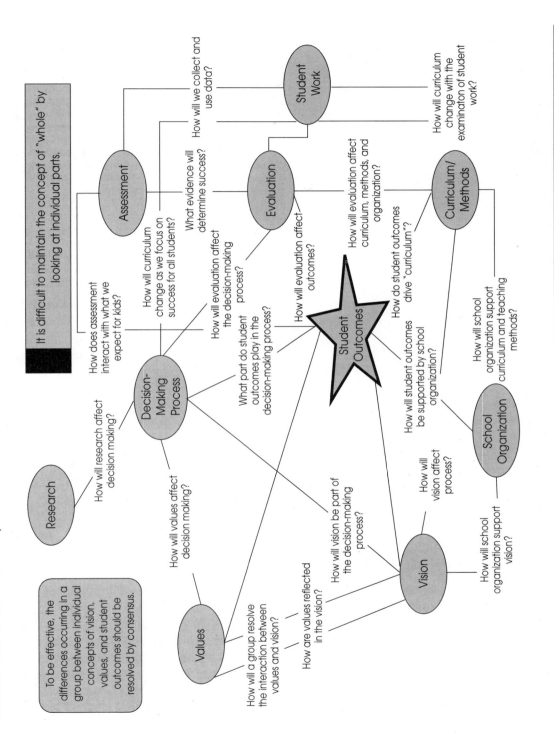

To be effective, the differences occurring in a group between individual concepts of vision, values, and student outcomes should be resolved by consensus.

It is difficult to maintain the concept of "whole" by looking at individual parts.

Research

How will research affect decision making?

Decision-Making Process

How will values affect decision making?

How does assessment interact with what we expect for kids?

Assessment

How will curriculum change as we focus on success for all students?

What evidence will determine success?

How will evaluation affect the decision-making process?

Evaluation

How will we collect and use data?

Student Work

How will curriculum change with the examination of student work?

How will evaluation affect curriculum, methods, and organization?

How will evaluation affect outcomes?

What part do student outcomes play in the decision-making process?

Student Outcomes

How do student outcomes drive "curriculum"?

Curriculum/ Methods

How will student outcomes be supported by school organization?

How will school organization support curriculum and teaching methods?

School Organization

Values

How will a group resolve the interaction between values and vision?

How are values reflected in the vision?

How will vision be part of the decision-making process?

How will vision affect process?

Vision

How will school organization support vision?

FIGURE 3.9

Mind Mapping Overview

BACKGROUND: Mind Mapping is based on early research showing left- and right-brain dominance for linear and holistic operations, respectively. Tony Buzan created the techniques of Mind Mapping® to support creativity and memory, and to deepen these links of creative functions to logical operations. Buzan's model has specific graphic techniques for Mind Mapping that support memory, expansion, and depth of concepts, and for readability so that collaborative problem solvers may more easily share their maps. Although Buzan suggests that learners share common techniques, he also emphasizes the development of personal style in mapping.

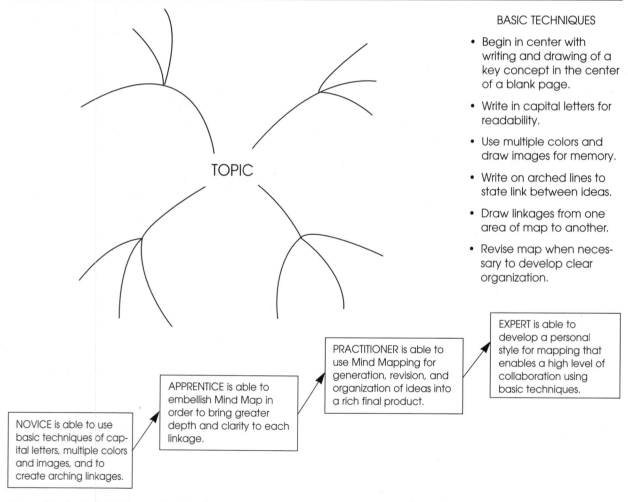

BASIC TECHNIQUES

- Begin in center with writing and drawing of a key concept in the center of a blank page.

- Write in capital letters for readability.

- Use multiple colors and draw images for memory.

- Write on arched lines to state link between ideas.

- Draw linkages from one area of map to another.

- Revise map when necessary to develop clear organization.

TOPIC

EXPERT is able to develop a personal style for mapping that enables a high level of collaboration using basic techniques.

PRACTITIONER is able to use Mind Mapping for generation, revision, and organization of ideas into a rich final product.

APPRENTICE is able to embellish Mind Map in order to bring greater depth and clarity to each linkage.

NOVICE is able to use basic techniques of capital letters, multiple colors and images, and to create arching linkages.

Source: Hyerle, D. (1999b). *Visual tools video and guide* (p. 5). Lyme, NH: Designs for Thinking. Copyright © 1999 by David Hyerle.

texts. So often in school we talk about finding out what students already know (facts and conceptual understandings). Yet in concrete, practical terms, there are few efficient and effective ways to assess their knowledge base.

As discussed in the previous chapter, a simple K-W-L is a starting point, but this linear list of "bits" of knowledge does not help students represent relationships and conceptual knowledge. Mind Mapping and other visual tools offer students "think time" for showing what they know in an interrelated form so that teachers may quickly review their cognitive map. New information may be introduced that fills in the factual or conceptual gaps in students' thinking, thus saving teachers and students a great deal of time.

Book Reviews

One very practical example of Mind Mapping is found in "Mapping Inner Space," a simple format for reviewing books or textbooks. Notice the emphasis on the metaphor of "viewing" rather than "reporting," as a student can uncover all of the pertinent details and conceptual linkages on a single page. This document thus becomes a guide that could be used as a supporting graphic for an oral or written presentation of the book (see Figure 3.10). As students create their own catalog of book reviews, they can begin to compare different books with greater ease simply by scanning their Mind Maps. They can see both the big picture and details for each book. The information is much more accessible and interesting in visual form compared to wading through pages of text to find links between books.

Students can also use this type of book review for studying content-area textbooks. So often when students take notes on chapters of a history, science, or mathematics book, they have difficulty seeing the interrelationships among all of the concepts that accumulate or evolve over the course of a text, or a text for a course.

The Mind Mapping technique supports students in making notes. By making a drawing of each chapter of a textbook, at the end of a term they can synthesize the information from multiple maps into a big-picture view of the subject matter. This big-picture map helps student construct and see both the forest and the trees, thus assimilating new knowledge with prior knowledge, chunk by chunk, or territory by territory.

MindManager Software

But what are the implications for lifelong learning? Businesses are now using Mind Mapping more than ever as a tool for creative thinking, problem solving, and communication of ideas internally within a group or as presentations to clients. A new software package called Mind-Man® (short for MindManager®) uses Buzan's techniques and many more to create a multidimensional tool for the business world. Here is an illustration of the software in practice, written by Bettina Jetter, one of the creators of the program:

Putting MindManager to Work
BY BETTINA JETTER

A winery in California has won a long-term contract to supply custom-labeled wine to an Asian company. The president needs to brainstorm the project with a partner currently in Europe and the marketing manager in South Carolina. They will require capital expenditure and new employees. Should they go ahead with the project?

First, the president uses MindManager to set out the pros and cons of the project and to establish priorities. As the software opens, she begins by plac-

FIGURE 3.10

A "Mapping Inner Space" Book Review

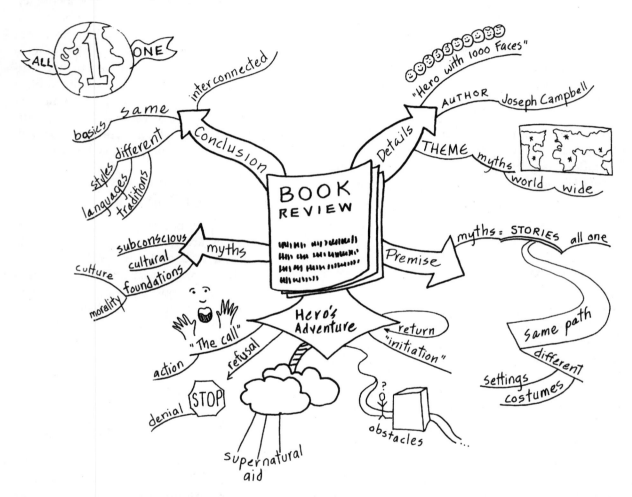

Source: Margulies, N. (1991). *Mapping inner space*. Tucson, Ariz.: Zephyr Press. Copyright © 1991 by Zephyr Press. Permission to publish granted by Zephyr Press, P.O. Box 66006, Tucson, AZ 85728-6006.

ing the company logo in the box centered on the screen. Then she enters their thoughts directly onto the screen, creating branches and sub-branches representing varied thoughts. She watches as the map gives structure to these ideas.

She rearranges the map by dragging-and-dropping items to a new location. She color-codes priorities by highlighting top ones in red, lesser ones in blue; adds follow-up steps; and shows relationships by drawing in arrows. She establishes links to the company's financial information stored in Excel software, which can be opened later by double-clicking on the branch.

She uses the text-note feature (note pad) to add background information on the prospective client, cost of new equipment, etc., which can become hyperlinks to the vendor's web site when needed.

The president then uses the MindManager conference invitation feature to e-mail the partner and the marketing manager to set up a MindManager conference later that day. Because each of them has Internet access and the MindManager software, the conferencing is easy. Everyone sees the map the president has drawn and can make additions or changes, which are transferred to each other's map in real time. They can also use the chat window to exchange information or ask questions.

At the conclusion of the conference, each participant can print out the same revised version of the map. That way no one has to write a report, an efficient use of everyone's time! The president now has to make a presentation to the employees and to suppliers, based on the map on which the management team has just been working. By right-clicking on the relevant branch, she connects with the "focus on topic" feature, which shows only those steps she wants them to see. The employees don't have to see the whole scenario. The map can be printed out as a one-page handout for a quick overview or as a detailed outline containing the conferees' text notes.

To reach her suppliers, she uses the company web site feature; a click on a few buttons on the toolbar creates the basics for a web site featuring the new project and makes all the relevant information available.

Everyone involved has a clear, graphical picture of the prospective expansion and a good understanding of his or her role in it. The use of color and images has brought the project to life,

without forcing the team to think sequentially and risk losing someone's attention on the way!

Mindscapes

More than a few educational and corporate trainers are using clustering, Buzan's Mind Mapping techniques, and generic brainstorming tools. Many teachers and students are also beginning to use Inspiration and other mapping tools in classrooms. Although they facilitate open-mindedness, often these tools do not reach into the rich area of metaphorical reasoning. A technique developed by Nancy Margulies (1991) called "Mindscaping" provides learners from classrooms to boardrooms with a fun and rigorous approach to constructing a metaphorical picture of complex information.

Here is a unique insight into Nancy Margulies' thinking as she formed the idea of Mindscaping from Buzan's early work on Mind Mapping:

> I found myself moving away from the rules and creating maps that had no central image (gasp!), more than one word on a line, and other rebellious inventions. . . . The name I decided to use is MINDSCAPES . . . landscapes of inner terrain. (p. 118)

There are unlimited forms of Mindscaping, though one model seems most productive for learners, site-based decision teams, and management purposes. The example given in Figure 3.11 was created by corporate trainer and expert in Mind Mapping Joyce Wycoff and teams of workers from four divisions of the DuPont plant in La Port, Texas. Here Wycoff describes the outcomes desired from the management teams:

> They wanted the divisions to recognize that they had many issues in common . . . such as safety and quality . . . as well as their beliefs and values. I was invited to help them brainstorm ways to develop, visually represent, and communicate a shared vision. In

54

FIGURE 3.11

Mindscaping Overview

BACKGROUND: Techniques for Mindscaping have come from many sources including Nancy Margulies, Joyce Wycoff, and Suzanne Bailey. The foundation for Mindscaping is in the metaphorical drawing of ideas and is most useful when attempting to see the big picture of an idea, vision, or outcome. Much as an artist has an image in mind for an idea, a learner identifies a concrete image in everyday life—such as a path, a building, or a plate of food—to represent both the conceptual basis and detailed interrelationships for an idea. Like any rich metaphor, it is important that the image is a clear metaphoric reflection of the idea rather than merely a placeholder for information.

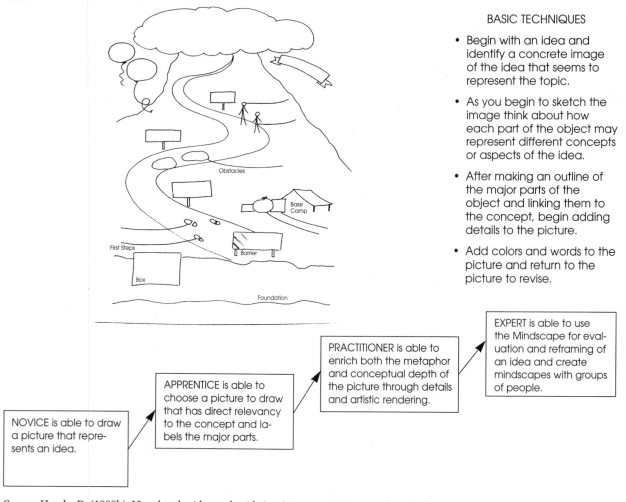

BASIC TECHNIQUES

- Begin with an idea and identify a concrete image of the idea that seems to represent the topic.

- As you begin to sketch the image think about how each part of the object may represent different concepts or aspects of the idea.

- After making an outline of the major parts of the object and linking them to the concept, begin adding details to the picture.

- Add colors and words to the picture and return to the picture to revise.

NOVICE is able to draw a picture that represents an idea.

APPRENTICE is able to choose a picture to draw that has direct relevancy to the concept and labels the major parts.

PRACTITIONER is able to enrich both the metaphor and conceptual depth of the picture through details and artistic rendering.

EXPERT is able to use the Mindscape for evaluation and reframing of an idea and create mindscapes with groups of people.

Source: Hyerle, D. (1999b). *Visual tools video and guide* (p. 6). Lyme, NH: Designs for Thinking. Copyright © 1999 by David Hyerle.

searching for a visual metaphor, we considered an underwater treasure hunt, a trip through outer space, a hike through the woods, and running along a race track. (Wycoff, with Richardson, 1995, p. 171)

As shown in the figure, the management teams chose a "trek map," with each symbol on the page representing key elements of this DuPont plant: four people for the four groups, boxes for the initial barriers to climb out of, a strong foundation at the bottom from which to begin, roadblocks as barriers and obstacles along the way, and a banner, trophy, and balloons signaling the final destination in the clouds.

This fundamental metaphor of everyday life—the journey—is especially rich and useful, as most people conceive of "life as a journey" (Lakoff and Johnson, 1999, pp. 193–194). This visual metaphor surfaces and makes concrete the interdependencies of a complex organism (the organization), and provides a way to synthesize overlapping ideals, belief systems, varying problem definitions and solutions. It also helps teams literally work together to draw out a common vision.

Seeking Personal Growth

As we close this chapter and open another, a key lesson may be learned from reviewing the webs of creativity presented in these pages: very simple graphics help learners and groups of learners represent and share evolving complexity, and through this complexity, seek a common vision. These tools also support inner understandings and open us to reflection. This reflection is prompted by looking down upon clusters, webs, Mind Maps, and Mindscapes of our own holistic making, much as we look at ourselves in the mirror or see our likeness on the surface of a pond.

This lesson has been revealed to me through the use of a brainstorming tool called the Circle Map, which I developed as one of eight Thinking Maps (see Chapter 6). I devised this tool to support learners in seeking the surrounding context in order to give definition to an idea or concept. The Circle Map purposefully suggests to learners that they do not immediate connect everything. Things may simmer a bit before connections occur.

After I drew a first version of the map—two concentric circles within a square—I looked down and realized it was, in fact, a pale reflection of an ancient form for self-reflection and personal growth: a mandala.

This simple map is one of the most powerful symbolic and spiritual representations for humankind—from mandalas used for centuries in India to the forms found on Native American shields. C.C. Jung used mandalas with his patients, asking them to draw out their thoughts, feelings, and intuitions in this format. Jung also spent many years experimenting with this form by waking every morning and creating a new mandala, expressively representing his own changes and transformations—as each of us has in our daily lives—as a kaleidoscope turning with every waking day into evening.

Jung goes on to identify the square (surrounding the concentric circles) as having four quadrants representing thinking, feeling, sensing, and intuition (Fincher, 1991, p. 134). From a Western perspective, Jung states: "The self, I thought, was like the monad which I am, and which is my world. The mandala represents the monda, and corresponds to the microcosmic nature of the psyche" (1973, p. 198).

The Circle Map in Figure 3.12 is by a student who was learning how to use Thinking Maps through a self-concept activity called "MYSTORY" (Hyerle, 1996). The information surrounding the

FIGURE 3.12

A Student's Circle Map About Her Life

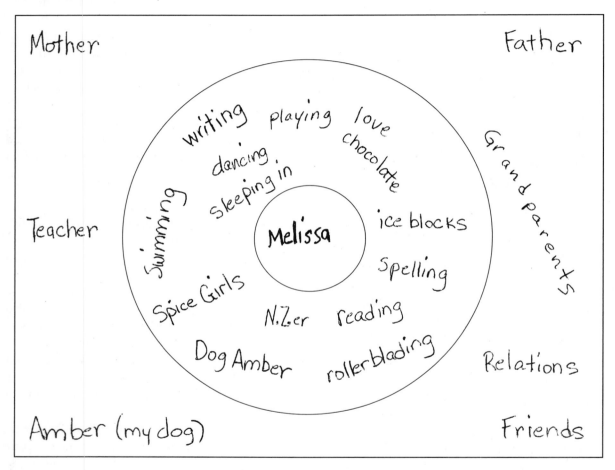

student's name is information from her life, and the information within the outside "frame" are the influences on her life. The Circle Map supports seeking and deepening associations and even metaphorical insights. Speaking of metaphors, Bena Kallick (1998) told me an example about using maps to understand metaphor (see Figure 3.13).

It is through the mandala that Jung also gained insight into a western view of the "self." In traditional Indian culture, mandala means center and circumference, a microcosm and connection to an ideal reality. Isn't it true that many of our beliefs, concepts, and actions are based upon some idealized view of how we want the world to be, rather than what it is?

FIGURE 3.13

Using Maps to Understand Metaphor

In a 12th grade English classroom, we explored the possibility of extending our writing through the use of metaphor. Students were asked to find a metaphor that appealed to them for use in an autobiography. They could pull it from any source.

One student came in with the line from Shakespeare's *Macbeth*, "Life is but a walking shadow." Although he intuitively liked the line, he was uncertain what it really meant. I asked the class to help him out. We placed a circle on the board and put shadow in the center.

I then placed an outer circle and asked everyone to brainstorm all of their associations to shadow. Once we did that, I asked the student if he had a better idea of what the line might mean for him. He immediately had an interpretation. We then placed the frame around the circles, and I asked him to try to give a context to the meaning of the line, first for Macbeth and, second, for his own life. The analogy was established and he walked off, eager to write.

—Bena Kallick (1998)

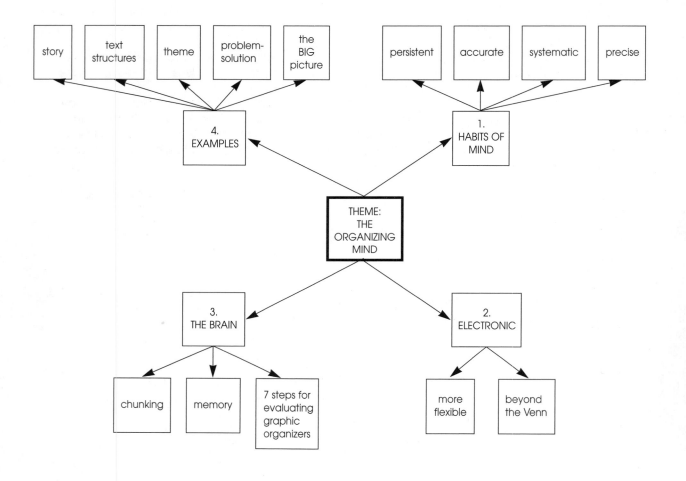

story

text structures

theme

problem-solution

the BIG picture

persistent

accurate

systematic

precise

4. EXAMPLES

1. HABITS OF MIND

THEME: THE ORGANIZING MIND

3. THE BRAIN

2. ELECTRONIC

chunking

memory

7 steps for evaluating graphic organizers

more flexible

beyond the Venn

The Organizing Mind

In any learning organization, things need to be organized, yet too much organization isn't necessarily the solution. We have all worked with some students and co-workers who cannot live outside the box of some pre-ordained organizational structure. They are trapped, and trap others, in a static world, when in fact the world is often messy and dynamic. This is the conundrum of the use of graphic organizers: too many organizers are handed out as fill-in-the-blank worksheets that actually may confuse students' thinking.

Our natural world has complex and stable organizational structures that are also in a state of transformation. This is best reflected by chaos theory, which posits that even within seemingly chaotic systems there are

No good teacher ever wants to control the contour of another's mind. That would not be teaching, it would be a form of terrorism. But no good teacher wants the contour of another's mind to be blurred. Somehow the line between encouraging a design and imposing a specific stamp must be found and clarified. . . .

. . . all so that the student may turn himself not into you but into himself. (Giamatti, 1980, pp. 28–29)

relatively stable structures and patterns. And so this is reflected in our lives. It is both the unique organizing structures and sensory systems of our brain and our conscious capacities of mind that enable us as human beings to slow the world down in order to make organizational sense of it. The organizing minds of our students are constantly learning new ways of both seeing and organizing the information taken in by the senses. Yet this process takes time—a lifetime for some! This is because as we mature and shift from job to job, or across content areas, we are learning about new and evermore complex organizational structures.

In this chapter we will investigate a wide range and uses of graphic organizers from useful starting points, or "templates," to "dynamic graphics." Unlike brainstorming webs, as we saw in the last chapter, graphic organizers are visual tools used specifically for organizing information in a very systematic way. Webs may lead to organizing structures, but always begin without a predetermined visual structure. Conversely, most graphic organizers begin with a relatively clear structure on a page or in the mind and are expanded according to the established pattern. This different type of visual tool thus becomes a focal point for facilitating a different array of habits of mind.

Organizers for Habits of Mind

Unlike webs, which facilitate "thinking outside the box," most graphic organizers are often structured so that students are supported in "thinking inside the box." A teacher may create or may find in a teacher's guide a specific visual structure that students follow and sometimes "fill in" in order to proceed through a complex series of steps. Often teachers match specific patterns of content or the development of content skills. Thus, I called them "task-specific" graphic organizers in *Visual Tools for Constructing Knowledge*.

Words of Wisdom About Graphic Organizers

Students in Suzanne Dobbs' history classes at Brethren Christian Junior and Senior High School in Huntington Beach, California, find graphic organizers (G.O.'s) to be welcome tools through which they can wrap their minds around the daily dynamic work of schooling. After reviewing their Web site on graphic organizers (http://home.earthlink.net/~tsdobbs/go.htm), I asked for their words of wisdom. Here are a few:

G.O.'s give you something to do, like drawing and coloring, while the whole time you're actually studying!
—*Joel Lazo Jr.*

When I was studying off of my G.O.'s. I realized that it was a lot easier than studying out of a book, almost like using a really good outline.
—*Carin O'Hara*

G.O.'s are easy to study from because they pick out the main ideas and all the details so you can do well on the test!
—*Jaime Knowles*

I like G.O.'s because I can take school work and change it into something I like.
—*Billy Roberts*

I just look at it and know exactly what I'm studying and why to study.
—*Mia Fatticci*

I like to design G.O.'s. It is more fun and easier to study from them than reading your book or notes.
—*Amanda Juarez*

These highly structured graphics may seem constraining at times, yet fruitful for many students who have trouble systematically approaching a task, organizing their ideas, and staying focused (especially when the task is complex). For example, many organizers are sequential, showing the guiding steps for solving a word problem, organizing content information for a research report, learning a specific process for a certain kind of writing prompt, or for a "story board" highlighting essential skills and patterns for comprehending a story. Because these types of visual tools are highly structured, they directly facilitate several habits of mind: persistence, self-control (managing impulsivity), accuracy, and precision of language and thinking. Figure 4.1 shows a bubble map of habits of mind for using graphic organizers.

Review most any graphic organizer—found in a textbook or teacher created—and you will find that the visual/spatial structure guides students through the steps, box by box, or oval by oval. Teachers report that one of the main outcomes of using task-specific graphic organizers is that they provide a concrete system and model for proceeding through a problem that students would otherwise give up on because they have not developed their own organizational structures for perseverance. An obvious reason is that the visual structure reveals a whole view of the process and, importantly, an end point.

This kind of structuring also provides some visual "guidelines," much like a rope they can hang onto, rather than impulsively jumping outside the problem to what Benjamin Bloom called "one-shot thinking." The visual modeling thereby shows students that they can decrease their impulsivity and stay "in the box" when they need to focus on following through to a solution.

This kind of modeling also lends itself to greater accuracy and precision of language and thinking. Oftentimes students don't have a record of their thinking—the steps and missteps along the way—and have a hard time differentiating one idea from the next. By capturing their ideas along a visual train of thought to a solution, students can look back on their ideas and refine them, and share their ideas with others for feedback.

Graphic Organizers: Reflections and Futures Uses

Before delving into the vast array of organizers, let's get an overview of these tools from a master of the trade, Greg Freeman. As a teacher, curriculum coordinator, and technology expert, Greg has used a wide range of these tools and

FIGURE 4.1

Bubble Map: Habits of Mind for Using Graphic Organizers

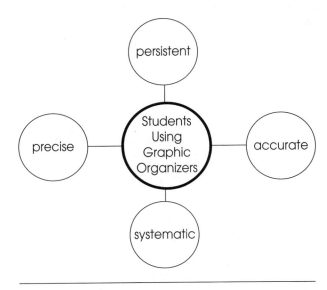

has a bigger picture about these tools and technologies for the 21st century. He now supports a Web site specifically developed to share graphic organizer applications (www.graphic.org). Here is a window into the future (that is already here!), provided by Greg Freeman:

An Overview of Graphic Organizers

BY GREG FREEMAN

A graphic organizer is a visual representation of concepts, knowledge, or information that can incorporate both text and pictures. The true value of such organizers is in the mind seeing visual patterns and relationships and deriving new insights from the patterning of the information. The pieces of a graphic organizer are much like the pieces of a jigsaw puzzle. When the strange pieces are put together they form a familiar picture. The individual pieces have no meaning, but the constructed puzzle does.

They have been used for many years as a visual tool for gathering, sifting, sorting, and sharing information in many disciplines. Early childhood teachers use Venn diagrams to teach comparing and contrasting objects, and engineers use complex organizers to develop new processes and simulations. They are easier for humans to understand than other representations such as pure text. They allowed the mind "to see" and to construct meaningful patterns to create new insights.

The research and power of graphic organizers is well documented in education. However, they were difficult to develop and time consuming to produce and edit. Most were templates, workbook-generated versions more often than teacher-generated ones. Until now, graphic organizers such as concept maps, radial diagrams, and note-taking matrices required careful planning and editing to avoid being cluttered, confusing, and consequently—unusable. They became unwieldy and not very user-friendly. The generation of a new idea

or an unanticipated change necessitated a complete remake of the map, diagram, or matrix. Furthermore, the map was often limited to the size of the paper and time allocated to generate the organizer. Think about your personal calendar!

Consequently, the organizer and the developer lost their creative power to collect and generate ideas and information—bogged down by erasers, space limitations, and capabilities to edit. Graphic organizers were bound by a "typewriter mentality" and cumbersome paper, pencil, and eraser. These problems kept the applications limited in scope and use to all but the most sophisticated user. Recent development of software to produce and edit graphic organizers has opened up new vistas for uses in gathering, sifting, sorting and sharing information in visual forms, yet unexplored. Barriers have been removed.

Newly developed electronic organizers and multiple windows ease designing, gathering and rearranging information. They allow the developer to cut, clip, paste, move, and rearrange information at will. Not having to preplan, draft, and remake brings into being the free flow of creativity and information in a natural manner. In view of the wealth of information (info glut?) and continued development of the Internet, a new and powerful tool, the electronic graphic organizer, can help plan, gather, sift, and sort the vast amount of information generated in cyberspace.

The use of hierarchical graphic organizers as a Web site navigation tool is appearing more frequently in Web site development. Internet search engines are incorporating graphic organizers as a tool to lead info seekers in their quests for information.

Chunking, Memory, and the Organizing Brain

In the previous chapter on brainstorming webs, we saw that webs and mindmaps almost always start in the center of the page and flow outward, radially, drawing out and linking associations with few rules to be guided by. Obviously, these relatively conscious associations being made are actually quite sluggish compared to the linkages each association is making deep in the unconscious, internal functioning of the brain. While brainstorming webs are commonly understood as based on associative logic, most graphic organizers are often derived from formalized processes. These organizers build capacity in students in their abilities to consciously "chunk" information.

From the mid-1950s on, we have believed that the brain automatically associates bits of information into "7 plus or minus 2" *chunks* (Miller, 1955). This chunking is now getting a tremendous amount of attention as present brain research reinforces behavioral research, especially as it supports the transfer of information from short- to long-term memory. Chunking happens unconsciously as the brain grapples with new information and as it pulls up information from long-term memory. Chunking may also be consciously engaged and may be improved when teachers introduce graphic organizers into the classroom in a *meaningful* way.

Bromley and colleagues (1995) present seven filters, or steps, for evaluating the usefulness and meaningfulness of graphic organizers in their book *Graphic Organizers* (see Figure 4.2). It is only through the chunking of information that we can get hold of infinitesimal and infinite actions of the brain, the stream of consciousness. When students chunk information, they are transforming it into a formalized array of information. Graphic organizers have been so successful because these tools create a logical *and spatial* arrangement of the chunks of bits of information on the page rather than students having to do all of the chunking in their minds.

The active chunking of information onto a page is much like constructing a constellation from a sky full of stars. Students can scan information, make sense of it, and see the pattern that the teacher is helping them connect. They can remember the visually chunked information better this way *along with* the auditory chunking that occurs when a teacher delivers information through a lecture or in lines of text written on the front board.

Robert Sylwester makes this point as he relates chunking to the curriculum:

> The curriculum enhances this remarkable brain capability when it focuses on the development of classification and language skills that force students to quickly identify the most important elements in a large unit of information. (Sylwester, 1995, p. 93)

In designing curriculum, publishers, curriculum directors, and teachers usually "chunk down" the content. We normally start with the big themes and break them down into manageable, smaller chunks. Heidi Hayes Jacob's work with mapping curriculum is a good example of this process (Jacobs, 1997). Much like a tree, the concepts are at the top, with the details organized into a foundation or a branch and root system of smaller chunks, and then coordinated in a sequential flow over the course of the year. The delivery of information—often through textbooks—is often lead by this kind of design. What Jacobs and others are doing with curriculum mapping is attempting to link the relatively independent content sequences into a big picture for teachers across a whole school or district.

Unfortunately, many concepts and ideas are presented to students in a deductive, pre-processed fashion with no clarity about the big picture of how it all fits together. At some point, these maps need to be shared with students! Carol Jago, a teacher at Santa Monica High School, explains this point well in the box on page 65.

FIGURE 4.2

Evaluating Graphic Organizers: Seven Steps

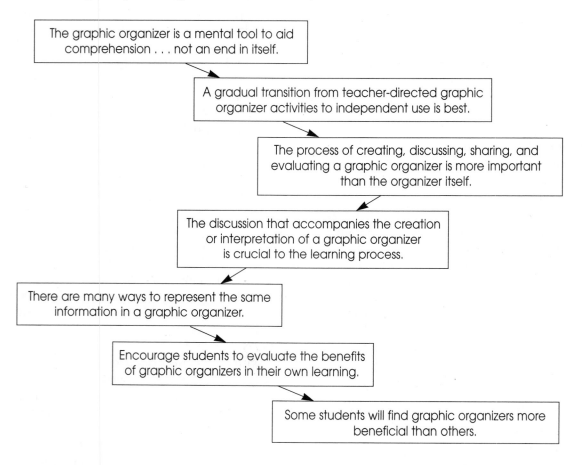

Adapted from Bromley, K., Irwin-De Vitis, L., & Modlo, M. (1995). *Graphic organizers* (p. 28). New York: Scholastic.

The organizing has already been done by the textbook, the teacher, or the computer program. By and large, students are supposed to see the big picture on their own and are rarely given the tools to put it all together other than through a test of their discrete knowledge. The students are asked to "learn" the information in a deduc- tive way: take notes, memorize the information as organized, and give back the information in written or verbal form . . . in linear form.

So where do graphic organizers fit into this discussion? As Greg Freeman mentioned earlier, many of the early and present graphic organizers have been highly structured "advanced organizers" and "templates" for students to fit information into. These preformed graphics have been successful because they match the capacity and needs of the brain to pattern information, to move the information from short- to long-term memory, and to make the information more meaningful. While some students may find graphics helpful when confronted with complex tasks or concepts, the prestructured graphic *may* be just a more sophisticated tool for replication, not construction, of knowledge.

These tools are like training wheels for a child learning to ride a bike, useful in the beginning but downright clumsy and embarrassingly extraneous in a very short time. We would not ask a 6-year-old who could ride a bike to keep the training wheels on, yet textbooks publishers and "graphic organizer" books continue to suggest that teachers have handfuls of duplicated graphics on hand for students to fill in.

When students become fluent with creating graphic organizers, they begin to control the information. They have the capacity to construct their own processes and visual tools for chunking information—and thus constructing knowledge. They move from strictly top-down, deductive reasoning, to bottom-up, inductive reasoning. They begin chunking up content and developing concepts.

> **I get lost easily, especially in my car. . . . Many children feel the same way about their journey through school. They navigate in uncharted, and in what to them feel like, shark-infested waters, waiting for the predators, sometimes called teachers, to attack. Teachers don't intend school to feel this way. We work hard to create lessons that make perfect sense to students, much as any map maker would take care with his drawings. Our lines are neatly drawn, the directions clearly marked, all major bodies firmly identified. The only problem is that we forget to tell the children that this is a map. . . . what students miss is the big picture. (Jago, 1995)**

From Static to Dynamic Organizing Minds

From all of the perspectives above—words of wisdom from students and Greg Freeman, brain research, and Costa's habits of mind—the mantra that may come to your mind about graphic organizers is that these are *tools* and not just *templates*. Next we will look at some of the best ways of systematically bringing these frameworks into classrooms so that not only are students not bored by staying within the lines, but they are guided to seek key relationships upon which they will be evaluated. In the past few years, major publishers have fully integrated graphic organizers into developmental reading programs. Though some of these graphics are positive additions, many are merely placeholders for information, more sophisticated ways of having students replicate information.

Figure 4.3 lists seven warning signs that you can use as an evaluation filter for previewing these graphics in basal programs and textbooks, and for using graphics in your classroom, school, or district. Many of these locks on student thinking create boredom, are time-consuming, and prevent students from engaging their minds. The structure is so rigid that there is no escape from the graphic.

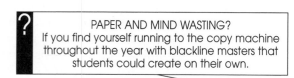

Seven Warning Signs That Graphics Aren't Working

? PAPER AND MIND WASTING?
If you find yourself running to the copy machine
throughout the year with blackline masters that
students could create on their own.

? FILL-IN THE BLANK, REPETITION?
If you find yourself handing out the same graphic
organizer without the students ever going outside the
lines, or if most of the organizers are of one type.

? ISOLATED?
If you find that there is no coordination of
organizers, then your students may never see
how different patterns work together.

? TOO MANY AND NOT TRANSFERABLE?
If you find that students have been given too many organizers—
in many different disciplines—they will begin to see that these are
not their tools to learn in depth but templates to fill in.

? TOO CONFUSING?
If your students continuously have to go back to the organizer
for instructions, it may be that there are too many actions
required for making sense of the information (break it down).

? NOT COOPERATIVE OR CONSTRUCTIVE?
If you find that the instructions for the graphics are that students fill in the
information and turn it in as part of their assignment without discussion;
or if you lead a classroom discussion and there is one right answer.

? NOT EVALUATIVE?
If students are not being asked: How did this graphic help or hinder
your performance? How could you have created a different graphic
to meet your needs? Did this graphic constrain your thinking?

FIGURE 4.4

Advanced Organizer for 6th Graders

The Endocrine System

Gland	Location	Function	Hormones	Malfunction
thyroid				
pituitary				
(etc.)				

Source: Ogle, D. (1988, December/1989, January). Implementing strategic teaching. *Educational Leadership 46*, 59.

For the remainder of this chapter we turn to a range of different types of organizers, beginning with the conveyance of mental models through templates, to dynamic graphics and complementary technologies.

Task-Specific Graphic Templates

In the 1960s David Ausubel (1968) introduced the idea of "advanced organizers" into educational practice. These organizers did not need to be graphic. An advanced organizer could be a guiding question to help students organize ideas as they read through a text. Now most advanced organizers have become graphic in form, many prestructured by the teacher or textbook to specifically guide students to organize or process information in a certain framework. Some of these organizers are actually tables, matrices, or note-taking guides. For example, Donna Ogle (Ogle, 1988/1989) gives an example of a table given to 6th graders before reading a selection on the endocrine system (see Figure 4.4). Ogle's development of the K-W-L process works quite well with these kinds of graphics, as students can use it to fill in what they know in the chart, think about what they want to know, and reflect on what they have learned after reviewing their completed graphic.

Story Organizing is another form of advance organizer used in language arts. Figure 4.5 is a high-quality example of how an organizer can guide students through a series of questions that support analysis of multiple characters and their interactions, toward a synthesis and summary of a story. This graphic, which may be used in many ways from individual to group to whole-classroom discussion, obviously leads to a rich structure for a follow-up piece of writing. It is an excellent example of how a graphic representation of a teacher's verbal flow of questions is much more clear. Students are actually given the "road map" of questions through which they can

FIGURE 4.5

Story Organizer Overview

BACKGROUND: The story organizer or map is a generic tool used specifically for interpretation of fiction. Other organizers have been developed for analyzing specific tasks for reading a story, such as plot analysis and rising action, and character description, comparison of characters, and for identifying thematic structures. Story organizers such as the one shown below are used to support students in bringing as many of these aspects of the story analysis together on a single page. It reinforces for students that most of these dimensions of the story must be included in the interpretive process for a complete analysis.

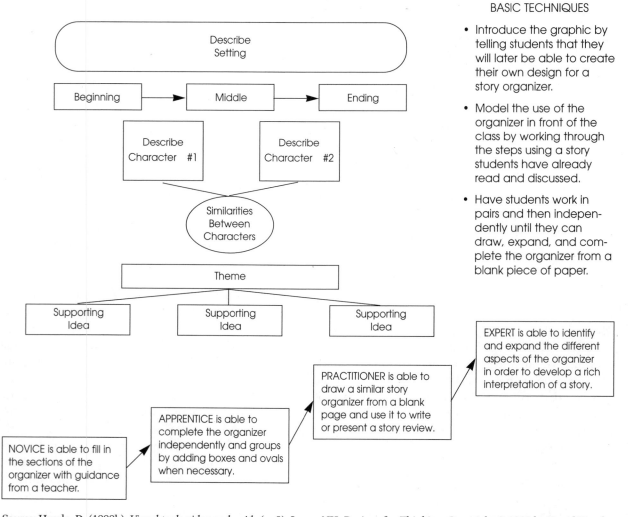

BASIC TECHNIQUES

- Introduce the graphic by telling students that they will later be able to create their own design for a story organizer.

- Model the use of the organizer in front of the class by working through the steps using a story students have already read and discussed.

- Have students work in pairs and then independently until they can draw, expand, and complete the organizer from a blank piece of paper.

Source: Hyerle, D. (1999b). *Visual tools video and guide* (p. 9). Lyme, NH: Designs for Thinking. Copyright © 1999 by David Hyerle.

see the whole process. They can see where the questioning is going, jot down responses, and *see* how the parallel questions about two different characters come together to form a rich analysis. More students per classroom will be able to follow discussions, stay on task, and be able to move to a higher level of comprehension with this road map in hand.

An infinite array of these "task-specific" advanced organizers can be produced. They are used in every discipline: from time lines in history to matrices in mathematics. Enough has been stated about the limitations of these tools, yet it should be restated, for comparative purposes, that these are static tools focused on a particular structure of information or flow of questions. Now let's look at more dynamic graphics from which students can expand their thinking.

Integrating Organizers, Text Structures, and Technology

Consider the implications of every student approaching a new text in any discipline with this question: *What is the structure of this text?*

If students could ask themselves—and answer—this question, they would have the comprehension capacity to decode the conceptual patterns embedded in any "wall of text." Here is the secret: all writing in fiction or nonfiction, literature or textbooks, is linear . . . and all of the conceptual patterns in the same pieces of writing are nonlinear (except for a pure narrative or step-by-step procedural instructions). Students need to ask themselves: Is the author structuring information by

- Making comparisons?
- Showing sequences?
- Making cause-effect arguments?
- Reasoning by analogy or metaphor?

- Hierarchical persuasion?
- Description or thematic approach?

Richard Sinatra's work using text structures shows how identifying them using a variety of graphic organizers provides students with specific tools for analyzing reading selections and for writing (Sinatra & Pizzo, 1992). Both hand-drawn and software-supported graphic organizers can be used.

The difference between Sinatra's work and typical use of isolated graphic organizers is that he systematically introduces students to a half dozen graphics that reflect basic reading text structures. Most applications of graphics focus on one or two isolated organizers, but do not provide extensive practice, application opportunities, and reflection so that students become fluent with these tools. Sinatra's design makes such fluency possible, providing students with a range of transferable advanced organizers. After systematic practice they independently gain an "organizational" menu of text types from which to analyze text and data-based information. These students are thus empowered to comprehend a range of different reading selections.

Sinatra fully integrates reading, text structure organizers, writing, and technology into a rich flow of steps toward full comprehension. Figure 4.6 is one example of how any teacher—in any discipline—can use graphic organizers as a foundation for learning at the beginning, middle, and end of a lesson.

As shown in this flow chart, Step 1 provides students with a thorough introduction to an array of text structures and possible graphic organizers that reflect specific patterns. Step 2 involves preplanning for the reading, which includes scanning the selection. In a particular lesson, a reading selection is provided on a topic such as food groups. In this case the students may be asked *predictive questions about the structure of the text* that help them identify the

FIGURE 4.6

Text Structures for Reading: A Nine-Step Process for Integrating Reading, Writing, and Computer Use

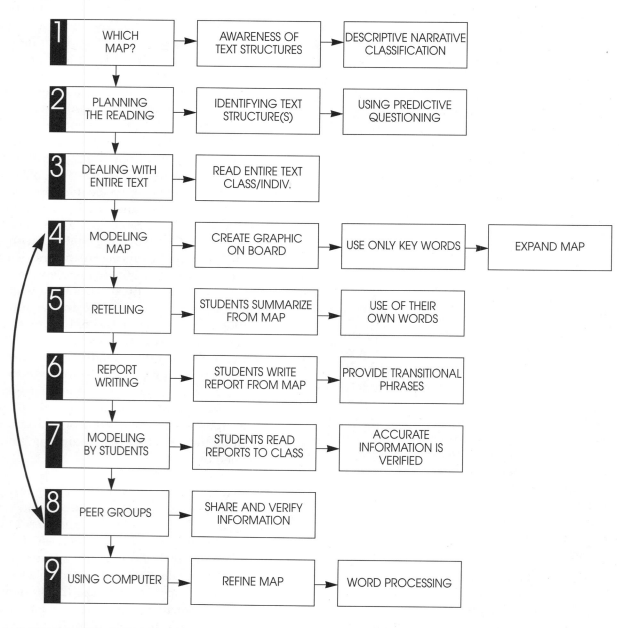

text structure. For example, "How many different types of food groups do you think there are?" This question supports them in thinking about the theme map and how the information might be organized (see Figure 4.7). Within this process, the students will have learned how to use the theme organizer as shown in Figure 4.7. This graphic organizer becomes the common element throughout all of the steps in the reading and writing process.

Steps 3 through 5 engage students in reading the text, filling in the graphic organizer, modeling the flexible creation of the graphic by the teacher, and verbalizing a summary from the completed graphic.

The teacher's use of the graphic in Figure 4.6 as a mediating tool for students to think about the text structure before, during, and after the reading is an effective model for using graphic organizers in any discipline. Additionally, these text structures, predictive questions, and the specific graphic related to each text structure are available to users of the Think Networks Software. This software has a systematic program for learning text structures. The only drawback is that it is not as flexible and user-friendly as other graphics software programs.

If the software has been used in Steps 1–5, then the complete graphic may be used as a structure for writing, reading, and group editing of a draft of the report in Steps 6–9. The software program, of course, is not the center of attention in this process: the software merely provides a high degree of structure within which students can practice specific text structures and then create them on their own by hand.

The extensive classroom-based research led by Richard Sinatra in New York City schools reveals very positive results. However, these results may be explained because the students have been systematically introduced to text-specific organizers, have received extensive modeling of graphics use, and have used the graphics in in-

teractive reading groups for writing with the support of both teachers and software. This use of graphic organizers for reading comprehension far exceeds the sporadic and relatively isolated uses of graphic organizers in basal programs and isolated applications in individual classrooms.

From Micro- to Macro-Graphics: Executive Processing Using Graphic Organizers

The graphic organizers we have viewed are focused mostly on specific tasks and text structures. These might be called "micro-graphics," or tools used by teachers and students to work out the *details* of the big picture. But what about the Big Picture? Many organizers—like our calenders or personal organizers—allow us to see and work through larger processes, from planning our year to research to problem solving.

In the Dimensions of Learning approach (Marzano, Pickering, et al., 1997), graphic organizers are presented across dimensions as suggested tools for acquiring and integrating knowledge (Dimension 2), extending and refining knowledge (Dimension 3), and for using knowledge meaningfully (Dimension 4). When used systematically, organizers are also keys to creating positive attitudes and perceptions (Dimension 1), because there is a greater clarity of processes, tools for collaborative learning, and high expectations for working with information. And, as highlighted in this book, graphic organizers have a direct impact on productive habits of mind (Dimension 5), as identified by Art Costa.

In the discussion of Dimension 4, use knowledge meaningfully, several organizers are presented for macro-processing, such as for general problem-solving steps (shown in Figure 4.8). Using organizers in this way gives students a flow of possible solutions and pathways back when

Theme Organizer Overview

BACKGROUND: The theme organizer is a generic form that has been developed and used by many teachers and curriculum developers. It is a key tool in Richard Sinatra's collection of text structures in the Thinking Networks approach and Sandra Parks' "Graphic Organizer" books. It is used as an organizer for reading comprehension across disciplines for supporting students in identifying a main theme, supporting ideas, and details. In this way, it is based on the cognitive skill of categorization, or the grouping of information. Students identify the main theme of a piece of writing and then group the key supporting ideas and details together into smaller boxes. Most often this organizer is presented to students as a blackline master.

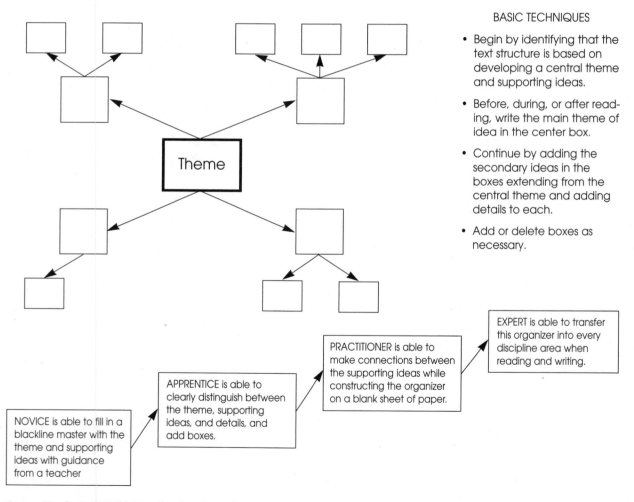

BASIC TECHNIQUES

- Begin by identifying that the text structure is based on developing a central theme and supporting ideas.

- Before, during, or after reading, write the main theme of idea in the center box.

- Continue by adding the secondary ideas in the boxes extending from the central theme and adding details to each.

- Add or delete boxes as necessary.

NOVICE is able to fill in a blackline master with the theme and supporting ideas with guidance from a teacher

APPRENTICE is able to clearly distinguish between the theme, supporting ideas, and details, and add boxes.

PRACTITIONER is able to make connections between the supporting ideas while constructing the organizer on a blank sheet of paper.

EXPERT is able to transfer this organizer into every discipline area when reading and writing.

FIGURE 4.8

Problem-Solution Overview

BACKGROUND: The problem-solution organizer was first researched in depth by Bonnie Armbruster in the area of reading comprehension. The example below is derived from Dimensions of Learning (ASCD). Problem solving is much more than this simple graphic, but the graphic provides a starting point for identifying goals and conditions and working through a problem. Importantly, there is a feedback in the system: The graphic shows the students that generating and trying out various solutions means returning to the beginning.

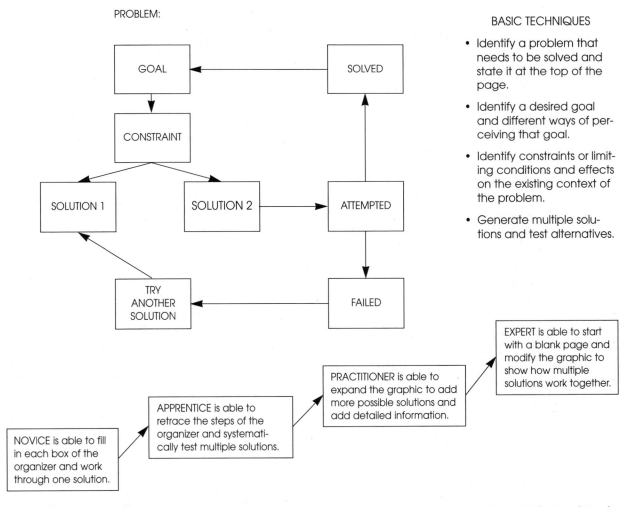

PROBLEM:

BASIC TECHNIQUES

- Identify a problem that needs to be solved and state it at the top of the page.
- Identify a desired goal and different ways of perceiving that goal.
- Identify constraints or limiting conditions and effects on the existing context of the problem.
- Generate multiple solutions and test alternatives.

Source: Hyerle, D. (1999b). *Visual tools video and guide* (p. 10). Lyme, NH: Designs for Thinking. Copyright © 1999 by David Hyerle.

a solution is not immediately apparent. This graphic is much like the templates shown earlier in this chapter and therefore not dynamic—unless brought to life through teacher modeling.

Another example of a template is the "Pathfinder" Research Template developed by Gwen Gawith (1987) from New Zealand (see Figure 4.9). It is amazing that on just one page so much graphic support holds together such a normally overwhelming process for students. There are only five steps, but along the way students receive facilitative questions, alternative pathways, sources to reference, suggestions for capturing information, and hints to get help when stuck within the process. Notice that within each step a question, rather than a to-do list, is offered.

Within this macro-organizer you also see a full integration use of different types of visual tools. Before Step 1, the students are asked to brainstorm ideas about the topic using mapping and to focus a broad topic "chunked down" by revising their map. Within steps 4 and 5 students are asked how they will organize and present the information, with sketches, diagrams, and charts. This research template, or Pathfinder, is a synthesis of a whole process, which includes diagraming templates, mindmapping, keywording templates for categorizing information, and presentation templates. While Gawith's *Information Alive!* booklet (1987) is out of print, her updated version, *Learning Alive!* (Gawith, 1996), for teachers of secondary students, is a rich extension and deepening of her first text on action learning.

Mapping Lesson Plans and the Big Picture

The research template just shown could well be used by students, teachers, administrators, and planners in the workplace. We already have ex-

amples of graphic templates used in schools for organizing, analyzing, and evaluating classroom planning and larger organizational structures called curriculum. Many different examples exist of lesson plan design tools that are graphically structured.

More recently, with the greater emphasis on complex integrated, thematic, or interdisciplinary curriculum designs, there has been a greater need for graphic representations. The Webbing Planning Sheet shown in Figure 4.10 begins with the identified theme in the center. The teacher then uses the template subject-specific applications and detailed language investigations to expand and link the theme through the disciplines. Whereas teachers usually use such graphic templates, students can also use them to record the array of activities surrounding the topics of "Change" and "Space." Students often need powerful tools like these because they reduce abstract, complex activities to a concrete and more simple representation. After going through a series of enlightening activities in an interdisciplinary unit, students are often left with no road map to show where they are going, how they are faring along the way, and how to reflect on the trip they have taken.

To map the big picture, students can use a research template, teachers (and students) can use an interdisciplinary design wheel, and teachers and administrators together can use detailed matrices for mapping the complex flow of curriculum from classroom to classroom, school to school in a district. In *Mapping the Big Picture*, Heidi Hayes Jacobs (1997) uses a graphic charting of curriculum as the central tool and organizing form for

• Collecting evidence of the existing state of what is being taught and when in a school or district;

• Analyzing the flow, connections, and gaps in the existing curriculum; and

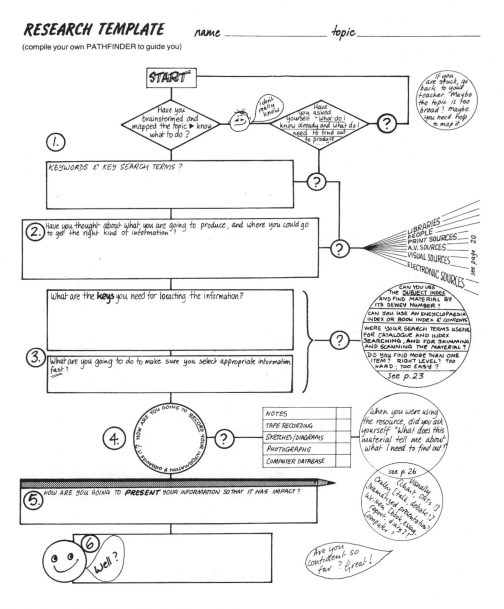

FIGURE 4.9

Pathfinder Research Template

RESEARCH TEMPLATE   name _____   topic _____
(compile your own PATHFINDER to guide you)

START

If you are stuck, go back to your teacher. Maybe the topic is too broad? maybe you need help to map it.

Have you brainstormed and mapped the topic ▶ know what to do?

I don't really know

Have you asked yourself "what do I know already and what do I need to find out need to produce

?

1. KEYWORDS & KEY SEARCH TERMS?

?

2. Have you thought about what you are going to produce, and where you could go to get the right kind of information?

?

LIBRARIES
PEOPLE
PRINT SOURCES
A.V. SOURCES
VISUAL SOURCES
ELECTRONIC SOURCES

see page 20

What are the **keys** you need for locating the information?

CAN YOU USE THE SUBJECT INDEX AND FIND MATERIAL BY ITS DEWEY NUMBER?

CAN YOU USE AN ENCYCLOPAEDIA INDEX OR BOOK INDEX & CONTENTS

WERE YOUR SEARCH TERMS USEFUL FOR CATALOGUE AND INDEX SEARCHING, AND FOR SKIMMING AND SCANNING THE MATERIAL?

DID YOU FIND MORE THAN ONE ITEM? RIGHT LEVEL? TOO HARD; TOO EASY?

See p.23

?

3. What are you going to do to make sure you select appropriate information fast?

4. HOW ARE YOU GOING TO RECORD YOUR INFORMATION & ORGANIZE IT?

?

NOTES	
TAPE RECORDING	
SKETCHES/DIAGRAMS	
PHOTOGRAPHS	
COMPUTER DATABASE	

When you were using the resource, did you ask yourself "What does this material tell me about what I need to find out?"

see p.26

5. HOW ARE YOU GOING TO **PRESENT** YOUR INFORMATION SO THAT IT HAS IMPACT?

Visually (Chart-Offs?) Orally (Talk, debate?) Dramatised presentation? Written, (book, essay, report, diary?) Computer?

6 Well?

Are you confident so far? Great!

FIGURE 4.10

Webbing Planning Sheet on Space

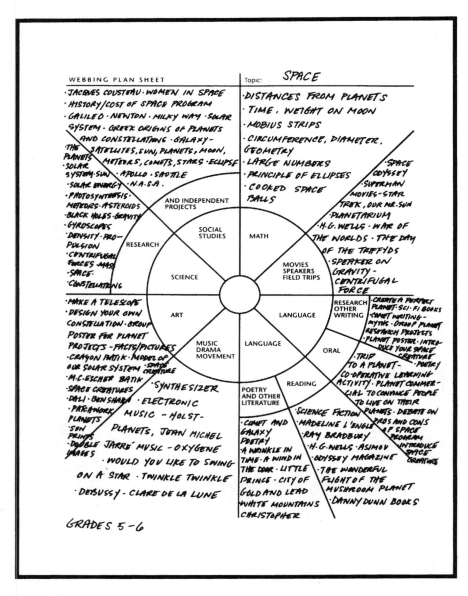

• Constructing new forms to systematically link curriculum and instruction.

The matrix that is established for constructing these different phases of analysis and problem solving is supported by a software program. This program brings a high level of organizational consistency and efficiency that otherwise would not be possible for taking on a complex systems problem.

No doubt this work is difficult, time-consuming, and an adventure into the politics of districtwide structures, especially when all of the stakeholders are included in the process. And it is hard to imagine being able to conduct this process without a graphic template and the software program that provides ease of entry, revision, and speed toward completion before participants bog down in details of the process.

Expressing Mental Models

In the past, writers within every field were quite comfortable expressing ideas in exclusively linear, written form—*even when their models were explicitly nonlinear*. Now, it is rare to proceed through a theoretical explanation without a graphic representation showing the complex, abstract interrelationships and interdependencies. As a matter of clear communication, these graphic mental models are almost a necessity and will become so as we progress in our graphic literacy.

Costa and Kallick (1995), for example, have at the heart of their book *Assessment in the Learning Organization* the concept of continuous growth through Feedback Spirals. The authors first describe these spirals in traditional linear form through pages of writing: variously, as internal, external, entwined, "grand" in design, enhanced with technology as well as immediate, long term, and some incomplete. They then synthesize this array of ideas and the com-

ponents and present them graphically in order to convey the model in a more concrete and dynamic form (see Figure 4.11).

The authors obviously grappled with whether what they were describing was the conceptual metaphor of either feedback "loops" or "spirals." Graphically, these two concepts look very different and show a rich pathway for readers. These

FIGURE 4.11

Continuous Growth Through Feedback Spirals

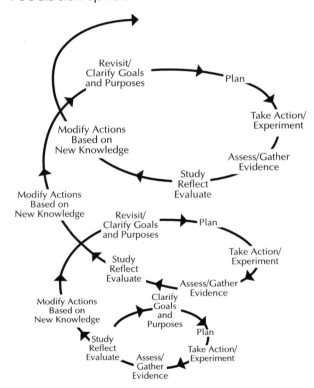

Source: Costa, A. L., & Kallick, B., eds. (1995). *Assessment in the learning organization: Shifting the paradigm*, p. 27. Alexandria, VA: Association for Supervision and Curriculum Development.

spirals show "a recursive process," something that is easily stated in written form and concretely understood through the graphic. This representation may have provided the authors a way to more explicitly represent nonlinear representations that they have explained in linear terms for both themselves and their readers.

What are the implications of this example for present students and for lifelong learning? If we want students to understand and express their conceptual and theoretical understandings within knowledge domains—and if we understand that these concepts are fundamentally nonlinear—

then we need to give them the graphic tools to show these models. Larry Lowery (1991), a leader in science education and stage development of thinking, provides a description and graphic example of an advanced stage (that all learners can attain) of Flexible Thinking (see Figure 4.12). Here the learner takes an organization structure such as a taxonomy and

> becomes able to develop a framework based on a logical rationale about the relationships among the objects or ideas in the taxonomy, while at the same time realizing that the arrangement is one of many possible

FIGURE 4.12

Example of Flexible Thinking

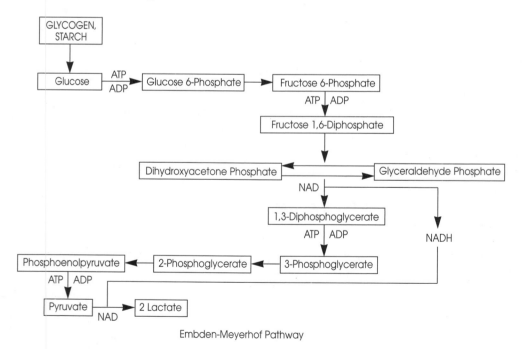

Embden-Meyerhof Pathway

Source: Lowery, L. (1991). The biological basis for thinking. A. L. Costa (Ed.) In *Developing minds: A resource book for teaching thinking* (p. 113). Alexandria, VA: Association for Supervision and Curriculum Development.

ones that eventually may be changed based on fresh insights. This stage of thinking can deal very flexibly with complex situations. Each field of endeavor produces new knowledge and further insights. Resolutions to problems and knowledge generation often take many forms. (Lowery, 1991, p. 113)

The emphasis here on arrangements, complexity, and forms of knowledge reveal that in order to think flexibly and gain new insights, students must be able to go well beyond textbook information in order to arrange (spatially) complex (linear and nonlinear) information into different (graphic) forms. Without graphic representations, most students' mental models will be stunted by a linear mass of information, a bare taxonomy chart memorized for the next exam.

Design and Understanding

As seen in this chapter, from micro-graphics for reading comprehension to macro-graphics for interdisciplinary and districtwide curriculum alignment, the design of graphic organizers is becoming an essential element to the successful representation of ideas. These are all "intelligent" tools. This chapter is no better summarized than by Jay McTighe and Grant Wiggins in their approach, "Understanding by Design." The graphic design templates that are key for others in applying their approach are tools for learning a process, and process tools for deeper understanding:

> Why do we refer to the template, design standards, and corresponding design tools as "intelligent"? Just as a physical tool (e.g., telescope, automobile, or hearing aid) extends human capabilities, an intelligent tool enhances performance on cognitive tasks, such as the design of learning units. For example, an effective graphic organizer, such as a story map, helps students internalize the elements of a story in ways that enhance their reading and writing of stories. Likewise, by routinely using the template and design tools, it is likely that users will develop a *mental* template of the key ideas presented in this book: the logic of backward design, thinking like an assessor, the facets of understanding . . . and design standards. (1998, p. 180)

Chapter 5 Overview

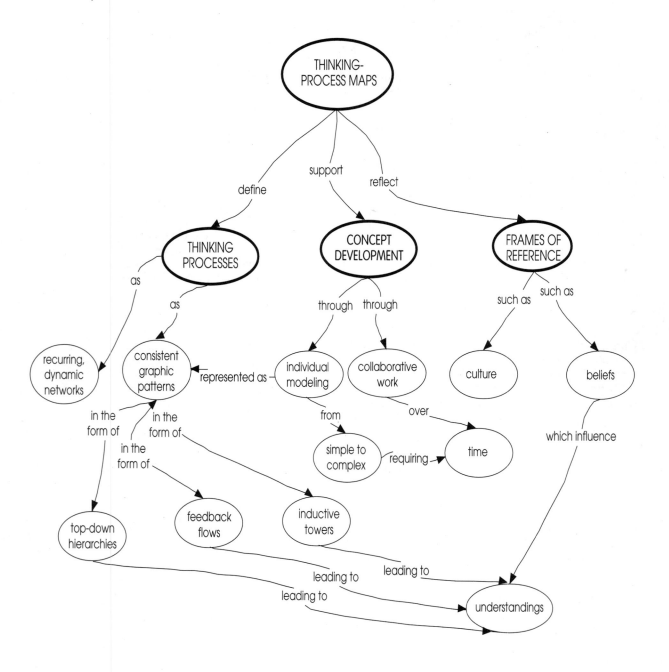

Thinking-Process Patterns

Thinking *About* the Box

As we saw in Chapter 3, brainstorming webs are used for thinking creatively "outside the box" of the daily classroom and workplace *mental* routines. These open webs help us to break mental and emotional barriers, reflecting the millions of rapid firing of associations occurring in your brain *as you read these words*. In Chapter 4, we saw that the preset flow charts, diagrams, and templates of typical graphic organizers help students think "inside the box." These tools, while often highly structured, also help students see a big picture by analytically organizing information. While this may be the teacher's framework and not the students' "big picture" or organizational structure, this graphic modeling within particular content areas supports the drafting of high-quality, and

Warning: Don't Judge a Graphic by Its Cover

Thinking-Process Maps often look much like some graphic organizers we see in classrooms, but the differences in the purpose, introduction, application, and outcomes are significant.

very specific, content outcomes. These graphics supply a mental safety net for many students, leading them into success and future independent applications.

There is a third way. A third kind of visual tool—called *thinking-process maps*—is in many ways an outgrowth and synthesis of brainstorming webs and graphic organizers. Different thinking-process maps are emerging in classrooms and the workplace for *simultaneously* supporting thinking "inside and outside of the box." Most important, these tools explicitly focus students' attention on thinking about the box itself, questioning what is influencing the creation of the box. Thinking-process maps systematically support teachers and learners in schools and workplaces by using recurring thinking patterns and reflective questioning. Figure 5.1 describes some of the functions of these maps.

FIGURE 5.1

Functions of Thinking-Process Maps

Thinking-Process Maps . . .

1. **Define** fundamental and specific thinking processes as recurring patterns.

2. **Support** expanding, applying, and transferring these patterns across disciplines.

3. **Guide** building simple to complex mental models individually and in collaborative working groups.

4. **Focus** on evaluating your own and others' thinking and models of concepts.

5. **Reflect** how your frame of reference influences your meaning-making, thinking patterns, and understandings.

FIGURE 5.2

Bubble Map Showing Habits of Mind Encouraged by Thinking-Process Maps

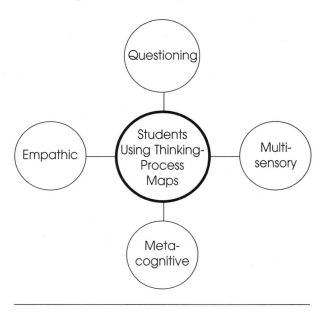

These practical and conceptually elegant tools are theoretically designed to reflect and generate recurring patterns of thinking, from fundamental cognitive skills such as comparison, classification, and cause-effect reasoning, to integrated visual languages, as we shall see below, such as concept mapping, inductive towers, and systems diagraming. While thinking-process maps scaffold many habits of minds related above to brainstorming webs and organizers, they focus explicitly on different forms of concept development and reflection, facilitating four habits of mind: questioning, multi-sensory learning, metacognition, and empathic listening (see Figure 5.2).

Through thinking-process maps, students are consciously asking themselves these metacognitive questions: How am I perceiving this system? What senses or inputs am I using? What thinking skills am I using? What frame of reference (or mental model) is influencing how I am patterning this information? What are some other ways of seeing these patterns? Where are my blind spots?

These metacognitive questions lead quite naturally and consciously to empathic understanding. Preeminent within the processes of concept mapping, systems diagraming, and Thinking Maps (Chapter 6) is the practical understanding that every person may create a different mental model based upon his or her prior knowledge, multiple frames of reference, and conceptual understandings. Empathic understanding—as a reciprocal process—requires not merely the self-less recapitulation of another's thinking and feeling, but a deeper sense of linkage and interpretation between the map in your mind and the map being expressed by another within the multiple frames of reference influencing these maps.

When Thinking Became Popular

Making sense of thinking-process maps requires context building in order to be understood as significantly different than brainstorming webs and graphic organizers.

During the mid-1980s "thinking" became popular in schools. While this sounds odd, a history of education in the Americas and most other countries around the world shows quite conclusively that the overlapping acceptance of behaviorism and static "intelligence" shaped an educational paradigm based on a "banking" system of learning, not the facilitation of thinking as we now understand it. During the week teachers delivered deposits of pieces of concepts, like pieces of silver, in discrete chunks, and students made withdraws through quizzes and tests. If the deposit was not learned, lessons were often repeated in the same format independent of learners' individual cognitive styles or the complexity of their unique capacities (Freire, 1970).

Of course, educators in schools should not be singled out because pedagogy is often framed by social and scientific paradigms of the past and not emerging ideas and theories. Change processes are slow; so many remnants (positive and negative) still inhabit classrooms of today. Educators are often constrained by the societal pressures of educating students for today's world and not educating based on prognostications of future needs. Now changes are happening quickly, so we must respond expeditiously and with greater care.

Before and during the early stages of the thinking skills movement of the past 20 years, the "brain-mind" was often called a "black box," an unknown and unknowable mystery. Breaking through the existing paradigm was the slow integration of process writing, problem-based learning, cooperative learning, and thinking skills in-

struction. An emphasis on thinking-processes led to a wide array of thinking skills programs in the 1980s, gave rise to a focus on higher-order questioning, and opened doorways to a constructivist view of learning and pedagogy.

Howard Gardner's view of multiple intelligences was the wave that broke open the static view of intelligence and gave voice and vision to different ways of thinking. Brain research has been a second wave, carrying us toward a new understanding of the complexity of cognition, learning, and human development. Along with brain research showing the emotional gatekeeping and filtering of the brain comes the third wave in the form of emotional-interpersonal intelligence (Daniel Goleman). As these waves of change influence classroom interactions, we can look back and see that the "black box" of brain functioning was central to how we envisioned human capacities and learning.

The foundation for the thinking skills movement was being built by cognitive scientists and developmental psychologists. One of the most influential of these pioneers was David Ausubel. Ausubel's research in concept development deeply influenced Joseph Novak's research and applications of concept mapping. In a new book on concept mapping for schools and corporations, Novak describes Ausubel's view of primary and secondary concepts (see quote in box on p. 84).

The distinction between primary and secondary concepts, by Ausubel's definition, is the difference between being able to actually touch and see concrete "ideas" and concepts that are abstract or invisible "ideas." These secondary concepts necessarily require *model building*. Models are representations of concepts that otherwise cannot be held in the hand for whatever reason. In a classroom, when a child creates a papier-mâché elephant, a sugar-cube model of an early California mission, or a styrofoam model of a molecular structure, a physical model is being

> Ausubel (1968) distinguished be-
> tween primary concepts and sec-
> ondary concepts. . . . Dog, mom,
> growing, and eating are examples
> of primary concepts formed by
> young children. As the child builds
> cognitive structure, he or she can
> acquire secondary concepts by
> the process of concept assimila-
> tion. Here concepts and proposi-
> tions in the child's cognitive struc-
> ture function to acquire new
> concept meanings including con-
> cepts that have no visible exem-
> plars such as molecule, love, and
> history. By school age, almost all
> concept learning is concept
> assimilation. (Novak, 1998, p. 41)

and idiosyncratic processes of learning. These tools provide a more concrete way to work with complexity, matching the capacities of our brains to see both the big picture and the details in both linear and holistic form.

As we look at these different forms, we will see that most require both consistent graphics *and* flexible use. This relationship matches, at the deepest levels, the structure *and* dynamism of the brain. We can see that the brain thrives on a consistent structure that easily evolves dynamically, as do fractals, toward novel configurations. With the most richly developed thinking-process maps, we see students thinking at micro and macro levels of performance.

Isolated Thinking-Process Maps

Much like the graphic organizers in the previous chapter, there are many clear examples of basic cognitive maps based on facilitating thinking skills. The most commonly used map is the Venn diagram, developed in 1898 by John Venn as a logic tool for showing category structure. It is important to note that there is confusion about the Venn diagram because teachers use it differently across disciplines for two different cognitive skills: categorizing and comparing. This is an unfortunate confusion because students will need to use this tool in mathematics for showing overlapping categories.

built. As much as we all talk about having such hands-on experiences for students, in practical terms, the physical creation of these models on a regular basis is impossible and ineffective.

Visual tools, and particularly thinking-process maps, are hands-on graphic, schematic *mental models* of concepts: students are able to draw the secondary concepts that they cannot hold in their hands. Because thinking-process instruction, technology, and problem-based learning demand conceptual development, visual tools are more necessary than ever. Thinking-process maps are visual tools based on representing conceptual growth, inductive and deductive development of concepts, systems thinking,

As shown in *Visual Tools for Constructing Knowledge*, (Hyerle, 1996, p. 77), Parks and Black (1992) have developed a range of these tools for categorizing, comparing, sequencing, and cause-effect reasoning. The repeated use of these forms—suggested for use as blackline masters—develop a specific way to apply these cognitive processes. By repeatedly using these forms—suggested as blackline masters—students can develop a specific way to apply these cognitive processes. This is a positive beginning because students develop automaticity in the skill, but the blackline masters should be used for introductory purposes and then discarded.

There are many other examples of these basic cognitive maps. James Bellanca has collected two dozen of these graphics in *Cooperative Think Tank I* and *II*. He shows in very explicit terms how to develop cognitive maps. Working with individuals and cooperative learning groups, he models the dynamism of the tool linked with interactive classroom thinking. For example, the "Fish Bone" is a long-used tool for collecting, organizing, and then linking causes to a single effect. Figure 5.3 shows the steps involved in using this technique with a group of students and provides an example.

> I used the fish bone because the shape looks really cool. . . . It really helped me study for the test. Graphic organizers are fun to make, and you remember a lot more than just reading books. The night before the test all I had to do was look over my fishbone.
>
> —Eric Proffitt
> 8th grader

By systematically modeling steps for students, starting with a blank page and building the map, teachers have no need for blackline masters, can facilitate individual and group work using a thinking skill and a cognitive map, and can use round-robin and voting processes to seek all possible answers and develop a synthesis graphic. Again, the difference between this cog-

FIGURE 5.3

Eight Steps for Using the Fish Bone and an Example

1. Identify the effect.
2. Identify the category names.
3. Use a round-robin to suggest possible causes.
4. Discuss the suggested causes.
5. Privately rank the causes.
6. Use a round-robin to make an unduplicated list of the causes.
7. Vote for rank order.
8. Prepare an explanation of the choices.

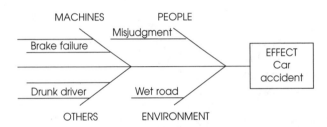

Source (for fish bone graphic): *The Cooperative Think Tank: Graphic Organizers to Teach Thinking in the Cooperative Classroom* by James Bellanca. Copyright © 1990 by IRI/ SkyLight Training and Publishing, Inc. Reprinted by permission of SkyLight Professional Development, Arlington Heights, Illinois.

nitive map and graphic organizers is this: students are learning and practicing a thinking skill in map form *in depth* that can be applied and transferred into every discipline, rather than using a graphic handed out by a teacher just a few times to learn a content skill or process, only to discard the tool and never use it again. With all the cognitive maps presented in this chapter, students are developing the "cognitive" skill along with the "map" for lifespan learning.

The Inductive Tower, one of the most conceptually rich cognitive maps, was developed by John Clarke (Clarke, 1991). There are many examples of cognitive maps based on hierarchical reasoning, which support students seeing the main idea, supporting ideas, and details on, respectively, the top, middle, and bottom of the map. Yet the top-down design also replicates the kind of deductive reasoning that we often ask of students and does not engage students in more generative, inductive reasoning. The Inductive Tower supports students in starting at the bottom of the page and developing conceptual categories as they proceed up the tower. Figure 5.4 explains how the Inductive Tower process works, as well as descriptions of students' abilities to use the process effectively. More in-depth descriptions of this cognitive map are in the first *Visual Tools* and in Clarke's book *Patterns of Thinking*.

> Concept maps are a tool for representing some of the concept-propositional or meaning frameworks a person has for a given concept or set of concepts. If a person could draw all possible concept maps in which a given concept is related to other concepts, for all possible contexts, we would have a good representation of the meaning the concept has for that person. This is obviously impossible. . . . none of us knows the full potential meaning for concepts we have because a new context or a new, related proposition could yield meanings we had never thought about before.
>
> (Novak, 1998, p. 40)

Return to Figure 5.1 (p. 82) as a guide for thinking about the qualities of concept mapping: *defining, expanding, building, evaluating, reflecting*. Now look at one student's work (see Figure 5.6) using concept mapping (Novak and Gowin, 1984; Novak, 1998). This student was fully trained in this process, starting with *defining* concept mapping as based on a theoretical view of thinking as primarily hierarchical. The student thus started at the top with the umbrella concept of "algebra."

This student was also flexibly *expanding* the concept map from the top down, with more inclusive concepts at the top and details below.

The interconnecting links within the maps give a visual tool for *building simple* mental models of algebra to a more complex, interdependent, holistic view of knowledge. This took not only an extensive amount of training, but obviously a whole year or more of algebra to facilitate this final configuration of concepts and details.

This student was also *evaluating* the development of the map throughout the year by way of a scoring rubric provided by teacher. As shown at the bottom, this concept map was given points by the teacher for the quality of "relationships," "hierarchy," and "cross links."

One of the key aspects of the use of concept mapping—not explicitly shown by this one example—is that students are constantly *reflecting* on the configuration of their maps, and thus

Concept Mapping

We now turn from more specific cognitive maps that are often used one at a time—such as a Venn diagram, a fishbone, or an inductive tower—to cognitive map languages, such as concept mapping. Figure 5.5 describes this process, as well as students' abilities to use it effectively. Concept mapping is more than a tool: it is a symbolic language, as Joseph Novak describes. There are many references to concept mapping as basically "webbing" concepts, but this term does not reflect the depth of this tool.

FIGURE 5.4

Inductive Tower Overview

BACKGROUND: The inductive tower was developed by John Clarke, Professor of Education at University of Vermont. The tower is based on inductive, hierarchical reasoning. Students are often asked to develop details about a topic starting with a main idea at the top of a map. This thinking-process map provides a tool for building categories or groups of ideas from an array of information at the bottom of the maps. Students then build the tower upward to the top. With each grouping at different levels of the map, students are constructing more inclusive and abstract concepts. At the top of the map is a generalization or category heading that represents the multiple levels of facts and inductively created concepts.

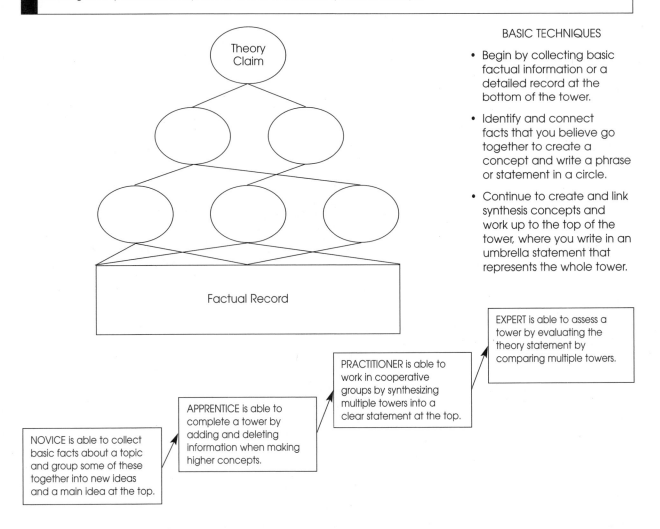

BASIC TECHNIQUES

• Begin by collecting basic factual information or a detailed record at the bottom of the tower.

• Identify and connect facts that you believe go together to create a concept and write a phrase or statement in a circle.

• Continue to create and link synthesis concepts and work up to the top of the tower, where you write in an umbrella statement that represents the whole tower.

EXPERT is able to assess a tower by evaluating the theory statement by comparing multiple towers.

PRACTITIONER is able to work in cooperative groups by synthesizing multiple towers into a clear statement at the top.

APPRENTICE is able to complete a tower by adding and deleting information when making higher concepts.

NOVICE is able to collect basic facts about a topic and group some of these together into new ideas and a main idea at the top.

Source: Hyerle, D. (1999b). *Visual tools video and guide* (p. 13). Lyme, NH: Designs for Thinking. Copyright © 1999 by David Hyerle.

FIGURE 5.5

Concept Mapping Overview

BACKGROUND: Concept mapping was developed by Joseph Novak and Robert Gowin, both of Cornell University. The term "concept mapping" is often used incorrectly as a generic term for any kind of semantic map, but as shown below the processes for using this tool have been systematically developed and researched. Novak and Gowin believe that concepts are linked together in the mind in a hierarchical system of relationships and interrelationships. New information is assimilated under an umbrella of more generalized concepts. The same array of concepts may be mapped differently and still be conceptually correct.

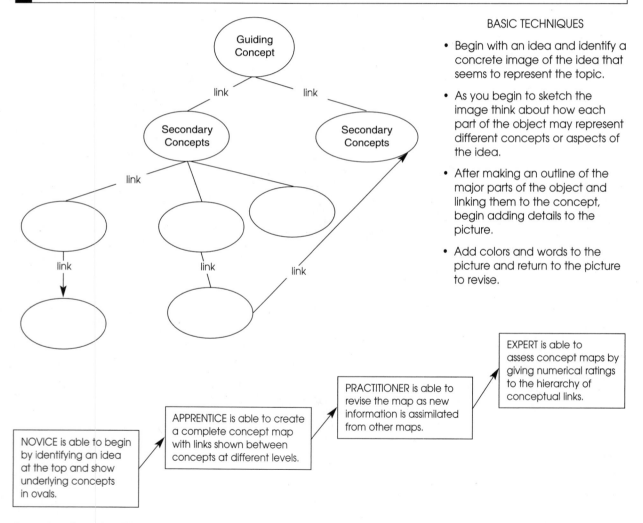

BASIC TECHNIQUES

- Begin with an idea and identify a concrete image of the idea that seems to represent the topic.

- As you begin to sketch the image think about how each part of the object may represent different concepts or aspects of the idea.

- After making an outline of the major parts of the object and linking them to the concept, begin adding details to the picture.

- Add colors and words to the picture and return to the picture to revise.

NOVICE is able to begin by identifying an idea at the top and show underlying concepts in ovals.

APPRENTICE is able to create a complete concept map with links shown between concepts at different levels.

PRACTITIONER is able to revise the map as new information is assimilated from other maps.

EXPERT is able to assess concept maps by giving numerical ratings to the hierarchy of conceptual links.

Source: Hyerle, D. (1999b). *Visual tools video and guide* (p. 12). Lyme, NH: Designs for Thinking. Copyright © 1999 by David Hyerle.

FIGURE 5.6

Algebra Concept Map Completed by a 10th Grader

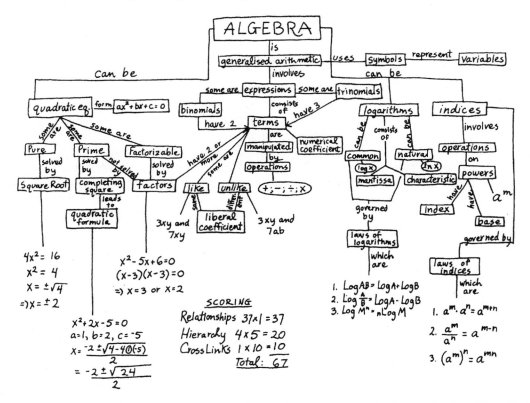

Source: Novak, J. D., & D. B. Gowin. (1984). *Learning how to learn* (p. 179). Cambridge, England, and New York: Cambridge University Press. Copyright © 1984 by Cambridge University Press. Reprinted with permission.

seeing how their frames of reference and mental models are influencing their perceptions.

While every student is ultimately responsible for his or her own concept maps, students are constantly comparing and sharing mapping information and their unique configurations. There is no ultimately "correct" map, as knowledge may be "correct" even when configured differently. Because of the flexibility of patterns of these multiple "correct" versions, Novak and Gowin called them "rubber maps," as they stretch in different ways to hold similar concepts or to find new understandings.

With just a glance, the algebra illustration may look like a well-developed mindmap, but it is an animal of a different kind. This is obviously *not* simply a rich brainstorming of what a student knows about algebra, but a highly evolved conceptual description. This explanation was possible only after a teacher and then this student were fully trained to make hierarchically interrelated links of concepts and details, starting from a blank page. The concept map shows that there are fundamental differences between thinking-process-cognitive maps and other forms of visual tools. This also shows the power of an elegant mental tool in the hand and mind of a student who has practiced this technique over multiple years. Software programs are now being developed based on concept mapping, such as Belvedere Inquiry Software. In Figure 5.7, Dan Suthers, a co-creator of the program, describes its uses. Figure 5.8 shows an example using the software to determine what might have killed dinosaurs.

These visual tools for mapping concepts are promising tools and technologies for investigation and concept development, and for lifelong learning in fields such as scientific discovery.

Because concept mapping and other thinking-process maps actually require training and support over time, it is not surprising that students are challenged to go beyond brainstorming ideas to more rigorous conceptual development of ideas. This is the case, as described by Paul Rutherford, a high school science teacher in Shawnee Mission, Kansas, who used concept mapping as a pre-post treatment assessment of students' conceptual understandings of Newton's laws of motion.

Concept Mapping in the Classroom

BY PAUL RUTHERFORD

My students resisted the considerable cognitive energy required to construct concept maps, at least from an individually constructed perspective. I journaled a number of their comments. One, in particular, I feel indicates the lack of real cognitive challenge that they had experienced prior to taking physics. One student said, "I have never had to think so hard before!" Yet another voiced a great deal of impatience, "Why can't you just give us what we need to know and forget this concept mapping stuff. It requires way too much thought and effort!"

FIGURE 5.7

What Is Belvedere Inquiry Software? by Dan Suthers

Belvedere was provided with a diagrammatic interface for cognitive, collaborative, and evaluative reasons. First, the cognitive: concrete representations of abstractions turn conceptual tasks into perceptual tasks. Thus the diagrams help students "see" and internalize these abstractions and keep track of them while working on complex issues. Second, the collaborative: diagrams support collaboration by providing a shared context and reference point. Third, the evaluative: student-constructed diagrams provide the teacher and the computer with a basis for assessing students' understanding of inquiry in general and of a topic area in particular.

Inquiry diagrams are useful for summarizing the overall trends in a complex debate. The visual depiction of ideas and relationships helps students "see" abstract ideas. The software can also help students get started by "prompting" them with empty shapes that need to be filled in with text. In our work with students, we have also found that inquiry diagrams can help students talk to each other about their project. Students can point to shapes on the screen to refer to ideas: "I think these two things together support this one." They can switch between working independently and working together with less effort and without losing track of what they are doing, because the diagram keeps track. For example, we have often seen a student work independently to find new evidence, then reinitiate discussion with the other student by pointing to her screen and saying, "I found something that contradicts this."

Students can begin with terms that make only the most basic distinctions, such as "data" versus "hypothesis" and "for" versus "against." As the need arises, more subtle distinctions can be introduced, for example, between problem, hypothesis, theory, prediction, data, evidence, conclusion, and so on.

FIGURE 5.8

An Example Using Belvedere Inquiry Software

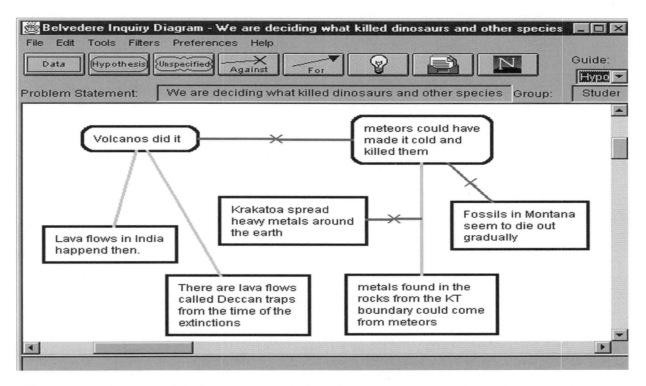

—Used by permission of Daniel D. Suthers, Assistant Professor, Department of Information and Computer Sciences, University of Hawaii at Manoa.

My students did receive mapping requirements with much more enthusiasm when they were required to map in groups of three. In fact, one article comes to mind in this regard, Wolff-Michael Roth's article in Science & Education (1994). On pages 9 and 10, he mentions that "justifying, explaining, and elaboration on claims thus became important structural supports for maintaining high levels of productive conversations about science topics." He infers that this social-development of scientific canon, is a most essential skill to be learned and collaborative concept mapping is a key avenue to build it.

For future practices, I will use concept mapping in a collaborative instructional vein. Not only are my students more inclined to enjoy and produce better results, but it is an avenue for practicing that all-important aspect of real-world scientific endeavors: bouncing ideas off of your team members. General Leslie Groves tried to extinguish that aspect of the Manhattan Project, yet J. Robert Oppenheimer convinced him of its absolutely imperative aspects for scientific research.

Feedbacks in the System

It is odd that we all work in school "systems," but few of us and fewer students ever fully learn how to *investigate* systems. We can talk about and blame "the system," tweak or shake up "the system" by making changes to specific parts, and totally transform larger sections of "the system" by symbolic acts or concrete decisions. We have also become quite fluent with talking about systems and feedback loops and change over time. This is a starting point for real change, but like the parable of the elephant that is touched by a half dozen blind men—each of whom believes he knows the whole animal by touching just one part—we are even further from the truth and lack the concrete tools to see the whole pattern as it exists *over time*.

Another form of thinking-process maps that is as elegant as concept mapping, yet based on "interdependent flows" and not "conceptual hierarchies" is *systems diagraming*. This approach is based on simple feedback loops and can be richly developed using **STELLA** software (Richmond et al., 1998). The background on systems thinking and **STELLA** software is taken up in detail in my *Visual Tools for Constructing Knowledge* (Chapter 5). For an overview, here is a simple diagram of feedback flows (see Figure 5.9).

This highly defined language of interdependent feedback loops helps students show and analyze mental models of dynamic systems: eco-, body, economic, political, social, and solar *systems* without having to rely solely on linear writing to convey interdependent systems.

A Feeding Frenzy

The key for understanding knowledge from a systems approach is recognizing "feedbacks" in a system. For example, during any given day we become hungry, and we feed ourselves. We make a choice of foods that are available, prepare and eat the food, and then the food begins to travel through our system. Both physical and psychological responses (or feedbacks) tell us that we are satisfied or not, and the instinctual fear of starving dissolves. As we eat more food we become comfortable as our body sends feedback signals, but if we eat too much food, the feedback comes too late as the body slowly becomes and feels bloated. Many different parts of the body system are at work in this process, centrally driven by the brain and performed primarily by the digestive tract. Of course, the nutrients, in the short and long term, have direct influences on the whole body and mind. Though some of the processes seem linear in form, this is not a linear process, as the body as system is responding dynamically to internal and external systems.

Furthermore, our whole body system is being driven by a mental model for eating. We have habitual practices that are framed by cultural influences, socioeconomic class, regional differences, and personal tastes. That most Americans eat meat, have three meals a day, have their heaviest meal in the evening, and that we now eat much more processed foods and "fast food" all influence not only when we get hungry, but what we desire to eat and where, such as in our cars. An example of the power of these mental models occurred when an Atlanta city councilman attempted to have "drive-thru" windows at fast food restaurants outlawed because the smog levels in Atlanta are so high. He believed that the idling cars and the mind-set of people not wanting to get out of their cars was both a real and symbolic influence on the overall problem. This example shows that systems are indeed connected in ever more complex ways: what and how we eat could directly influence specific parts of other systems, such as the air quality.

FIGURE 5.9

Systems Feedback Loops Overview

BACKGROUND: Systems feedback loops have been used in many fields to show cycles: a simple feedback loop that every elementary child learns about is the precipitation cycle. When students learn about predator-prey relationships and food chains, feedback loops may be used to show the dynamic interrelationships among the variables in a system. Systems Thinking as a way of understanding the world has evolved from business and industry applications in the 1950s and has gained visibility in the field of education through the work of Peter Senge of M.I.T. While systems thinking does not absolutely require mapping using feedback loops, it is hard to imagine representing a system and all its complex interdependencies other than through visual means.

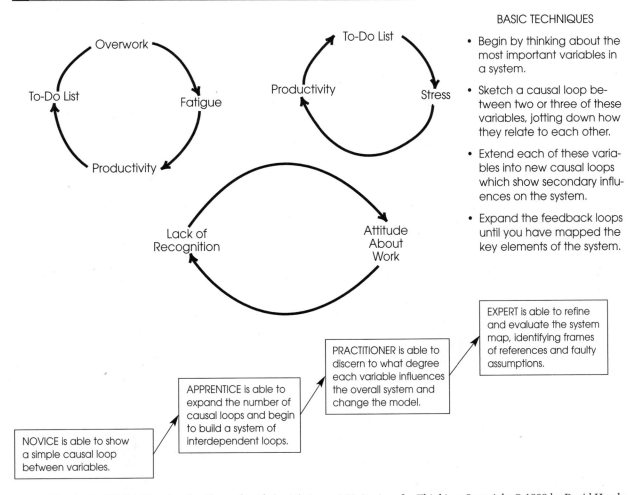

BASIC TECHNIQUES

- Begin by thinking about the most important variables in a system.

- Sketch a causal loop between two or three of these variables, jotting down how they relate to each other.

- Extend each of these variables into new causal loops which show secondary influences on the system.

- Expand the feedback loops until you have mapped the key elements of the system.

EXPERT is able to refine and evaluate the system map, identifying frames of references and faulty assumptions.

PRACTITIONER is able to discern to what degree each variable influences the overall system and change the model.

APPRENTICE is able to expand the number of causal loops and begin to build a system of interdependent loops.

NOVICE is able to show a simple causal loop between variables.

Source: Hyerle, D. (1999b). *Visual tools video and guide* (p. 14). Lyme, NH: Designs for Thinking. Copyright © 1999 by David Hyerle.

Importantly, what was just described was presented in a purely linear form, through a logical progression of sentences. In the linear attempt to describe the situation, I linked interconnected ideas and concepts grammatically, not spatially. The use of feedback loops and systems approaches results in a diagram of interconnections that is a graphic grammar for revealing interdependent relationships.

The "limitations of the linear" are revealed when we begin to create a visual representation of these intertwined systems. Let's look at a school that has systems thinking and diagraming as a central tool for learning, and how students took on the issue of hunger.

A Visit to a School "System"

Every school has implicit and explicit ways of nurturing learning and measuring progress. Often the differences from school to school are impossible to see. But at the Murdoch Middle School, Peter Senge's Five Disciplines are posted in every classroom and systems feedbacks—and the language of systems thinking—is used as a common thread for instruction and learning (see Figure 5.10).

Approximately 175 middle school students are housed in this innovative school located in the lower floor of a nondescript office building in Chelmsford, a suburb of Boston. The school's "charter" states that students leaving the school will be proficient problem solvers who

- Think systemically,
- Investigate options,
- Test mental models,
- Develop and ask relevant questions,
- Make informed decisions,
- Evaluate their process, and
- Apply their knowledge to real-world situations.

FIGURE 5.10

The Five Disciplines of a Learning Organization

Personal Mastery	Team Learning	Systems Thinking	Shared Vision	Mental Models
The discipline of continually clarifying and deepening personal vision, focusing energy, developing patience, and seeing reality objectively.	The discipline of "thinking together" and recognizing patterns of interaction that both facilitate and undermine a group's ability to learn and create together.	A framework for seeing interrelationships rather than things; to see the forest *and* the trees.	Common aspiration among people in the organization.	Deeply ingrained assumptions that influence actions.

—Adapted from Senge, P. M. (1990). *The fifth discipline: The art and practice of the learning organization.* New York: Currency Doubleday.

These aims are accomplished through many means, including full training for staff in systems thinking and diagraming and Peter Senge's Five Disciplines, a focus on interdisciplinary topics, and with accountability to the standards set by the State of Massachusetts Department of Education (see Figure 5.11).

Upon entering the school, meeting with principal Sue Jamback, and beginning a tour led by

FIGURE 5.11

A View from Murdoch Middle School
by Sue Jamback, Director

Murdoch Middle School in Chelmsford, Massachusetts, is committed to teaching middle school students challenging subject matter. We expect students to show evidence of comprehension and to demonstrate that they can apply sophisticated concepts in meaningful ways.

Traditionally, schools provide information to students, most of which is communicated verbally and supported with written text. This method of instruction is linguistically and linearly based. It assumes that learners are assimilating knowledge (thoughts and concepts) by hearing and reading. It does not provide students with a framework with which to physically manipulate or visually see their ideas as they are emerging.

We are using Systems Thinking and Systems Dynamics to support learning in each classroom. These concepts provide formal structure in the form of causal loops and physical models. Students can draw the models and loops. They use them to show changes over time, interrelationships and interdependencies, and cause and effect.

These are not simple concepts to grasp. Students, rather all learners, will benefit from drawing, labeling, and reorganizing information graphically. Acquisition of complex materials requires more than words.

two students, few things seemed different than in any other school. At the first turn, two teachers entered a classroom, asking for one of the students. "Whooooaaa!" roared a room full of typical 7th graders in unison, expecting the girl to be reprimanded. One of the teachers laughingly said: "You're going to have to check your mental models—we want to talk to her about an award she will be receiving." The classroom went silent.

Mental models have been described in many ways by linguists, cognitive scientists, and business management theorists and consultants. Basically, a mental model is the theory or framework that a person—or a group—has for *how a system or part of a system works*. It is a mind-set and overlapping frames of reference for how things or people act. In this example, the students knew the basic definition of a mental model, so when the teachable moment arrived, they were dealt a wake-up call: they had been going along blindly interpreting the situation without reflection.

This first step in systems thinking is an awareness that our prior experiences, knowledge, culture, and belief "systems" deeply influence what and how we learn new things. A system is not simple, and our mental models of it can reek havoc on our ability to see the whole picture and shift our insights out of poorly formed assumptions.

Systems thinking—as a modeling tool—asks us to build, challenge, and evaluate our mental models through feedback loops. At the time of this visit, Murdoch students were immersed in a unit on hunger. Several students were investigating India and the dynamics of hunger in this vast country. While most students also use brainstorming webs for generating ideas, systems loops and diagraming are, as one student said, "harder." For example, one 8th grader created a basic feedback loop to show one set of dy-

FIGURE 5.12

A Feedback Loop: India's Employment/
Nutrition Success by an 8th Grader at
Murdoch Middle School

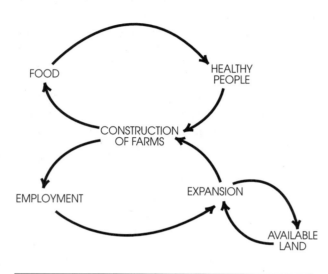

these variables. Matt defines a problem, then analyzes it using a linked array of loops. Ultimately, he offers a solution with its implications. Importantly, both of these students are analyzing interdependencies in the system, and their loops could be integrated as their analyses grow. David and Matt are not just attempting to name parts of the problems, but showing them in relationship to the whole system. In feedback form, these relationships appear much more complex, yet on another level the complexity is much easier to understand than if presented in a linear fashion. Of course, our most interesting and important problems are complex and exist in systems.

The visual mapping of systems through feedback loops is central to Murdoch School, so much so that they have developed a rubric for developing and assessing student portfolios (see Figure 5.14).

As shown in the rubric, the systems flows are linked to creative presentation of ideas, written narrative, and overall clarity. Also notice that the rubric includes an assessment of grammatical usage, spelling, neatness of presentation in the written text, along with clear drawings and appropriate labeling of the feedback flows. These feedback flows are the starting point for thinking systemically, but once these visual tools are used proficiently, Murdoch students incrementally begin using STELLA software to more deeply analyze whole systems.

It would seem odd if students, teachers, and administrators at the Murdoch School didn't also walk the talk of thinking systemically about their own environment and interactions, and, in fact, plenty of evidence illustrates that this form of thinking takes shape in the day-to-day lives of learners. House meetings are held regularly, where the whole school population gets together to discuss their needs. Because each person is part of the "system," if the school doesn't pay at-

namic relationships as a starting point (see Figure 5.12). The two central loops are mutually reinforcing: as construction of farms increases so too does food and, most likely, more healthy people. At the same time, new farms also create increased employment and expansion of land use. A "balancing" loop, in this case the available land, may have negative or positive influences on new construction.

Another student, Matt Lowe, created an extension of the problem of hunger in India. Rather than looking at supporting programs, such as the development of agriculture, Matt examined the problem of money being invested in nuclear testing (see Figure 5.13). Again, this is a starting point from which we can see a wide number of feedback loops linking into each of

FIGURE 5.13

A Feedback Loop: India's Nuclear Testing Effects by Matt Lowe, an 8th Grader at
Murdoch Middle School

PROBLEM
DESCRIPTION:
Nuclear testing is taking money away
from the poor people
who need it.

SOLUTION
SUMMARY:
Restrict nuclear material purchases
so that all that money can help
poor people.

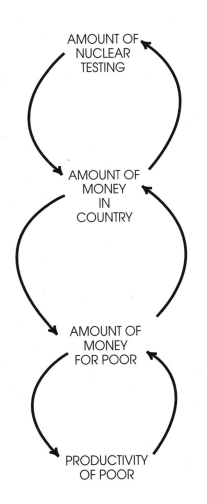

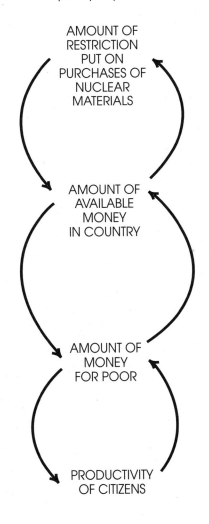

FIGURE 5.14

Murdoch Middle School's Feedback Loop Rubric for Developing and Assessing Student Portfolios

Category	Mastery	Successful	Emerging	Not Yet Successful
System thinking loops	• Multiple loops used and clearly defined action on causal loop. • Uses only nouns to show cause and effect. • Explains both +/- cause and effect. • All information is accurate and correct. • Problem is clearly presented.	• Demonstrates an understanding of balancing and reinforcing loops. • Loops marked correctly. • Information is accurate and correct. • Some insignificant errors.	• System loops contain some errors, but some evidence of understanding can be seen. • Some information and assumptions are accurate and correct.	• System loops are drawn incorrectly and/or not labeled. • Reinforcing and balancing loops are not correctly identified.
Written narrative	• Written narrative tells the story of what could happen in the loop diagram. • Tells the story of two opposite situations. • Clears up any confusion in causal loop diagram.	• Written narrative tells the story of one situation.	• Written narrative provides some ordered details about the loop.	• Written narrative shows little understanding of the causal loops or leverage points.
Overall clarity	Portfolio ready. • Clearly drawn and labeled, no verbal explanation required. • Creative presentation.	• No spelling errors and few grammar errors. • Clearly drawn, has most labels, some verbal explanation required. • Typed and neatly presented. • Turned in on time.	• Loops drawn with some labels. • Some spelling or grammar errors.	• Drawing not clear and sloppy, few labels. • Excessive grammar or spelling errors. • Missing work or late.

tention to each person, the whole system—not just the person—may suffer over time. For example, when one student in the school was diagnosed with severe allergic reactions to perfumes and scented oils, everyone in the school came to a consensus (the school runs on a consensus model for decision making) that no one in the building would wear scented perfumes, lotions, or cologne. While this systems approach *seems* an analytical way of understanding empathy, it may be a much deeper, more fully integrated way of understanding empathy than trying to reinforce "caring" in a school through character development programs.

Leaving Tracks

At Murdoch Middle School, issues such as attendance, conflicts, and behaviors among adolescents and adults in the building are often talked about with the language and the analytic understanding of the dynamics of complex systems and of the implications for behaviors, not just in the moment, but over time. Problem-based learning and real-world issues are thus extensions of the microcosm of this school in its attempt to understand systems.

One of the phrases that seems to embody this understanding—and that is heard in classrooms, meeting rooms, and hallways—is "actions leave tracks." This is much like the metaphor of throwing a stone into a pond and noting the ripple effect. But in the case of leaving tracks, consider systems thinking: actions often do not ripple for a short time, in a uniform way, and then disappear. The idea of leaving tracks is consonant with a new paradigm of science and with common sense: what we do may have profound effects in the short term and may forever influence future actions and behaviors across systems.

The leaving of tracks may be positive or negative. For example, that a whole school agreed to refrain from wearing perfumes left tracks in the short term by making one student feel welcome and be healthy. The process of this decision set a precedent about the importance of process, of relationships in the school, and for taking concrete actions in response to different needs within the school. This track will leave a trail for future years for students in the school, and in the future lives of many of these students.

The "leaving of tracks" also creates a metaphor for thinking systemically: that mental models can be traced and changed; that change happens over time; that change is complex with innumerable pathways, feedbacks, and flows; and that attempting to see the whole of an idea, concept, feeling, or action makes each part that much more important. It simply helps us realize that the whole *is* greater than the sum of its parts because of all of the interdependent relationships between and among the parts. These patterns as processes are what is worth thinking about.

6

Thinking Maps®
for Reading Minds

Uniting Processes, Products, and Assessment

During a recent presentation to their school board, two 5th grade students and their teacher Sarah Curtis used three Thinking Maps as tools to show their assessment of Thinking Maps as tools for learning at Hanover Street School in Lebanon, New Hampshire. On the front of the handout to the board, she wrote:

> As a 5th grade teacher, I am thrilled about the process and products that my students and I have demonstrated in response to the implementation of Thinking Maps. The best way I can convey the flexibility and vast utility of this language and set of visual tools is through their use. The following maps were generated by our 5th grade class as we thought about Thinking Maps. The type of map used is determined by the organization and thought processes behind the reflections.

Behind the reflections of these visual presentations by students is a richly evolved capacity showing that not only were these students using Thinking Maps for learning, but also as metacognitive tools for evaluating the efficacy of these very same tools. Figure 6.1 shows applications of Thinking Maps by teachers and students. Figure 6.2 illustrates how the use of Thinking Maps evolved from being entirely teacher directed to being a shared teacher-student responsibility, to students constructing their own maps.

As students such as these within whole schools become fluent with Thinking Maps, this array of eight visual tools becomes a common visual language for thinking, collaborative learning, curriculum design, assessment and self-assessment, and, most important, *continuous cognitive development* over an individual's lifespan of learning.

While educators are beginning to map the integrated alignment of content curriculum and skills beyond mere scope and sequence, there are few if any attempts—or even the understanding—that we must align the development of the most fundamental array of skills that will carry our students from kindergarten to college,

FIGURE 6.1

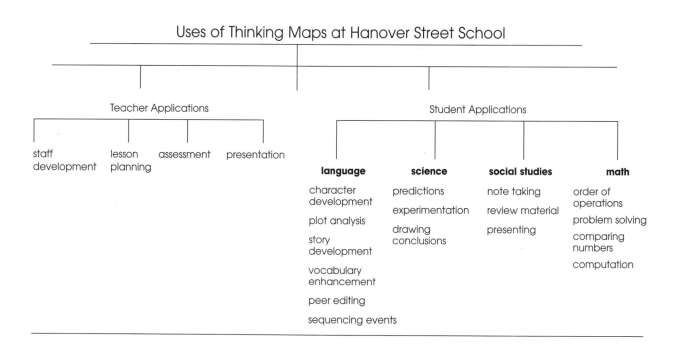

across multiple careers, and for lifespan learning: thinking skills. Most colleges now require critical thinking skills courses, probably because our schools have not yet systematically integrated these skills into the yearly flow of learning from kindergarten to graduation.

Students may exit our schools with the ability to read text, but not build meaning. Our students' *cognitive skills* development—the foundation of every school's goals or mission statement—are randomly supported, rarely raised to the level of fluency, and nearly absent as a distinct dimension of assessment. We now know that "information doubling" abounds beyond our students' capacities or necessity to learn all the new content. And, as we know from brain research, we must facilitate the *patterning* of content knowledge as a foundation for learning. Thinking Maps, as a language

of visual tools based on fundamental thinking skills, has been proven as one route for *unifying* content and process instruction, and assessment of products. Figure 6.3 provides a description of Thinking Maps.

Jeffrey Spiegel, the principal of Hanover Street School—where Sarah Curtis, her colleagues, and students have used Thinking Maps for several years—put it succinctly, "Thinking Maps are the glue that holds it all together."

Reading Texts

Human scholarship, and thus much of what is taught in schools, deals with our capacity to interpret texts. Imaginary characters abound in fictional texts, but in schools most texts are non-

FIGURE 6.2

How the Use of Thinking Maps Evolved at Hanover Street School

Teacher Directed	Shared Responsibility	Student Constructed
instructed in map choice	given appropriate map	assignment given
lead through map construction and word/thought placement	own map expansion on template	open choice for method of presentation
whole-class lessons	own thought placement	elect to use maps to share ideas
modeling	group or individual task	select appropriate map and construct to fit the needs of the task

fiction and data-based. Even so, students are still constantly *interpreting* for themselves the meaning of a scientific concept, a problem in mathematics, an ethical dilemma in social studies, a point in history.

In classrooms, the sources and forms of "texts" have changed. Log on to the Internet, open a new textbook, or access a CD-ROM, and you will not just see walls of texts—where strings of text blocks build one upon another—without graphic support in either picture or symbolic support. The pervasive use of graphics is now

unmistakable. With the wealth of information available in so many forms, we need to refine and maybe redefine what we call a "text." We need new tools that support the interpretation of information that comes to our students in different forms.

Texts are patterns of information, layered, found in many forms, and requiring interpretation. In fact, the idea of "reading" goes well beyond normal text. To be able to "read" a situation—such as a conflict in a cooperative group—is, in a symbolic sense, to read a text. Texts are all

Thinking Maps Overview

BACKGROUND: Thinking Maps is a language, or tool-kit, of eight thinking process maps, developed by David Hyerle. Each map is graphically consistent and flexible so that students may easily expand the map to reflect the content pattern being learned. Thinking Maps are introduced to students as tools for reading and writing, content-specific learning, and for interdisciplinary investigations. Over time, students learn to use multiple maps together and become fluent in choosing which maps fit the immediate context of learning. Thinking Maps and Thinking Maps Software are used in whole schools through faculty training and follow-up.

BASIC TECHNIQUES

- Begin with an application of each of the maps to a concrete object in order to understand the relationship between thinking processes and Thinking Maps.

- Expand each map to show big picture and then prioritize information by deleting ideas from maps for reading comprehension and writing.

- Use multiple maps together to construct related patterns of learning, and use "frame" to identify frames of reference.

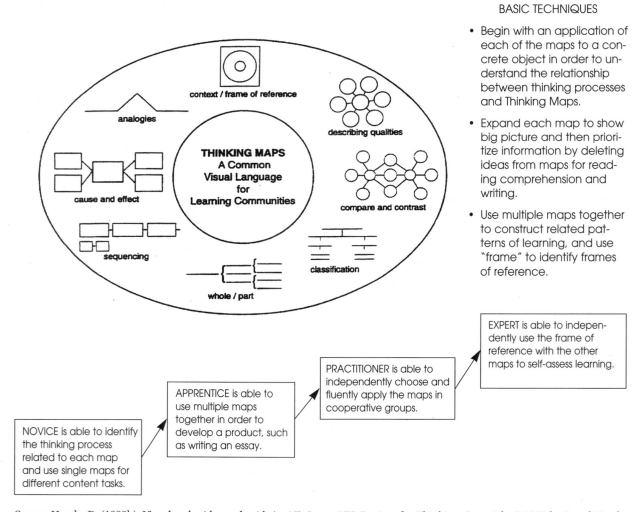

EXPERT is able to independently use the frame of reference with the other maps to self-assess learning.

PRACTITIONER is able to independently choose and fluently apply the maps in cooperative groups.

APPRENTICE is able to use multiple maps together in order to develop a product, such as writing an essay.

NOVICE is able to identify the thinking process related to each map and use single maps for different content tasks.

Source: Hyerle, D. (1999b). *Visual tools video and guide* (p. 15). Lyme, NH: Designs for Thinking. Copyright © 1999 by David Hyerle.

around us for us to read. Gary Synder—poet, teacher, and naturalist—may have found the origin of text and gives us a way of defining text in this new century (see quote in box).

> A text is information stored through time. The stratigraphy of rocks, layers of pollen in a swamp, the outward expanding circles in the trunk of a tree, can be seen as texts. The calligraphy of rivers winding back and forth over the land leaving layer upon layer of traces of previous riverbeds is text.
>
> In very early China diviners heated tortoise shell over flame till it cracked and then read meanings from the designs of cracks. It's a Chinese idea that writing started from copying these cracks.
>
> (Snyder, 1990, p. 66)

In schools, the texts are information stored through time and more formalized:

• The layering of story and poetry,
• Histories from different cultures overlapping,
• The current events of daily life winding together,
• Expanding numerical strings and traced circles,
• Molecular designs building fractal-like into new forms, and
• The outward expanding relationships between participants in a learning community.

Texts are information stored through time—often permanently in libraries and now often fleetingly on the Internet—and interpreted or "read meanings" by the minds of our students. Meaning is created through the interaction of the mind of each individual learner and these overlapping texts. When we are good at "reading situations," we have the capacity to shift from text type to text type, from cultural context to different contexts, and fluently "read" new situations.

Thinking may be understood as the capacity of the learner to read patterns embedded in text, much like the Chinese diviners reading the cracks of the tortoise shell in the Gary Snyder quote. And the process of thinking is the capacity to abstract from and construct concepts from the shards of stored information in the text overlapping with the stratified "prior knowledge" stored in the brain.

Reading Minds

From this discussion, we can now enter the ambiguity in the title of this chapter: "Reading Minds." Thinking Maps, as presented in this chapter, are tools for

• Students to mindfully "read" and interpret information,
• Teachers to "read" and assess their students' minds by the maps that they create,
• All learners—students and teachers alike—to "read" and reflect on their own minds and thus become self-assessing.

It is important to emphasize not only the application of these tools as shown for content and process learning, but also for use in the moment and summary assessment of basic knowledge and conceptual understandings.

Visual tools of different sorts have been presented in this book as patterns for making sense of our own stored knowledge and to assimilate new information and concepts. So it is reasonable—practical—to consider how these tools could be synthesized, coordinated, and organized in a meaningful way for learners. This is the idea behind a common visual language of Thinking Maps.

These eight patterns of thinking are designs that expand, overlap, and layer information for making meaning (Hyerle, 1988, 1990, 1991, 1993, 1995, 1995/1996, 1996). This language of thinking-process maps is in many ways a synthesis of each of the three types of visual tools presented in this book. As a *language* of visual tools, each of the eight Thinking Maps embodies the generative quality of *brainstorming webs*, the organizing and consistent visual structure of *graphic organizers*, and the deep processing capacity and dynamic configurations found in *thinking-process maps*. At anytime learners can access this thinking tool kit—using it on paper or through software—to construct and communicate networks of mental models of linear and nonlinear concepts.

The Thinking Maps were created during the generative stage of my writing a student workbook for facilitating thinking skills (Hyerle, 1988) and as a model is analogous to the key or legend of symbols you will find on a typical road map. Each graphic primitive is a unique starting point for mapping thinking. But why only eight maps? I became aware that fundamental thinking skills (Upton, 1960) might be more easily understood as a visible, concrete *pattern of thinking*, not merely an abstract skill performed solely "in the head" and represented by writing or speaking. Each map is based on, respectively, one of eight fundamental human cognitive processes identified by cognitive scientists from Piaget to present times.

While there are *only* eight maps, there is an infinite number of configurations of each map, much like the English language, which has *only*

26 letters in its alphabet but a vast number of combinations. Five essential qualities of Thinking Maps are key to seeing how these tools are infinitely expandable and used simultaneously, as a carpenter would use multiple tools for constructing buildings (see Figure 6.4).

These qualities of each tool lead to more complex orders of thinking, such as evaluating, thinking systemically, and thinking metaphorically. When students are given common graphic starting points, *every* learner is able to detect, construct, and communicate different types of patterns of thinking about content concepts.

After participating in Thinking Maps "basic training," conducted over a year's time, teachers and students become independent and coopera-

FIGURE 6.4

Bubble Map of Five Qualities of Thinking Maps

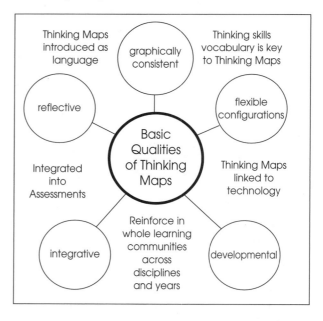

tive tool users, fluently linking content knowledge and working together to build maps on the way to final products. At this writing, over 1,000 whole school faculties have had in-depth training and follow-up coaching in these tools. Teachers, students, and administrators report some or all of these outcomes after using Thinking Maps over time:

- Increased memory of content knowledge when reading,
- Well-organized final products, particularly written work,
- Deeper conceptual understandings,
- Greater capacity to communicate abstract concepts,
- Heightened metacognition and self-assessment,
- Enhanced creativity and perspective-taking, and
- Transfer of thinking processes across disciplines and outside school.

These outcomes are also supported by test results in reading, writing, and mathematics. Some of these results are discussed in the next sections in context (for details, please see Appendix A, p. 134).

Reading, Writing, and Researching Using Thinking Maps

The remainder of this chapter will focus on practical applications of Thinking Maps. Thinking Maps are used for reading comprehension across disciplines. The training manual *Thinking Maps: Tools for Learning* (Hyerle, 1995) contains content correlations and examples of Thinking Maps applications to mathematics, science, social studies, reading, and writing. As a filter for what follows, here is a "quick correlation" to the area of communication skills (see Figure 6.5). While each map is based on a defined thinking-

process, teachers and students use this correlation to fully integrate the reading, writing, and thinking connection necessary for full comprehension and expression of ideas.

Use this correlation to think about the processes and products discussed in the coming pages: phonemic awareness for young children in Los Angeles, research using Thinking Maps Software by a 1st grader after a visit to a North Carolina zoo, research on a famous African American by a 5th grader in New York City, an analysis of Julius Caesar by a 9th grader from Los Angeles, a closer look at lesson planning using essential questions as applied to social studies research in a New Zealand classroom, and successful reading comprehension for adult literacy in a junior college in Mississippi.

Phonemic Awareness

The great debate in education of this passing century has been between "content" and "process" teaching. The most recent derivation of this fractious, dichotomous argument is between phonics and whole language. This debate is much like the Sufi parable from the first page of this book: it has prevented us from seeing another side, and the deep connections between the two, which will help solve the problem. In this new century, educators will be looking for theoretically grounded and useful practical models as tools that explicitly integrate content and process instruction, including phonemic awareness and comprehension.

Sasha Borenstein, director of the Kelter Center, works closely with the Los Angeles City Schools and with teachers all over California in the area of literacy development. The Kelter Center staff work with students who need to master "the basics." And what are the basics? As Sasha draws from her direct experience and research

FIGURE 6.5

Quick-Reference Content Correlation to Eight Thinking Maps for Communication Skills

Circle Map
- Representing and brainstorming ideas
- Defining words by showing context clues
- Identifying audience and author's point of view

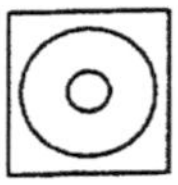

Bubble Map
- Expanding descriptive vocabulary
- Describing characters using adjectives
- Providing descriptive details for writing

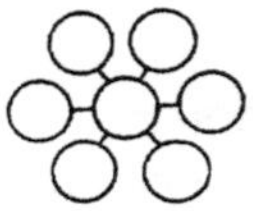

Double Bubble Map
- Comparing and contrasting characters
- Prioritizing essential characteristics
- Organizing a compare-and-contrast essay

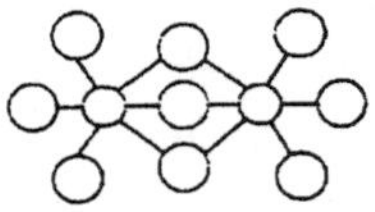

Tree Map
- Identifying main idea, supporting ideas, details
- Organizing topics and details for writing
- Taking notes for lectures and research papers

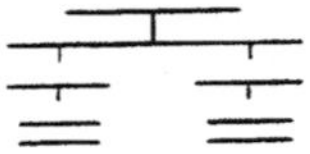

Brace Map
- Comprehending physical setting in stories
- Analyzing physical objects from technical reading
- Organizing and writing technical manuals

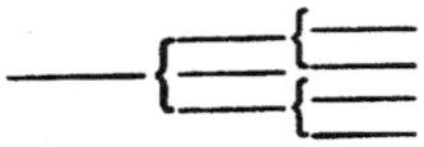

Flow Map
- Sequencing story plot by stages and substages
- Analyzing and prioritizing important events
- Sequencing paragraphs for writing

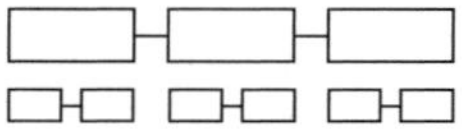

Multi-Flow Map
- Analyzing causes-effects in literature
- Predicting outcomes from previous events
- Organizing "if-then" persuasive writing

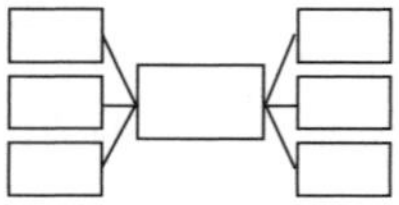

Bridge Map
- Comprehending analogies, similes, and metaphors
- Preparing for testing using analogies
- Developing guiding analogies for writing

Source: Hyerle, D. (1995). *Thinking maps: Tools for learning* (Section 3, p. 4). Raleigh, NC: Innovative Sciences, Inc. Copyright © 1995 by Innovative Learning Group. All rights reserved. Used with permission.

with students and teachers, we find that the basics are supported by using Thinking Maps as bridges between phonemic and metacognitive awareness. (Words in bold are the explicit cognitive skills being facilitated using Thinking Maps.)

Phonemic Awareness and Metacognition

BY SASHA BORENSTEIN

The recent research in the area of literacy done by the National Institute of Child Health and Devel-

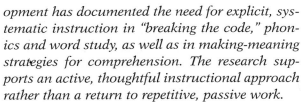

opment has documented the need for explicit, systematic instruction in "breaking the code," phonics and word study, as well as in making-meaning strategies for comprehension. The research supports an active, thoughtful instructional approach rather than a return to repetitive, passive work.

Thinking Maps are flexible, active tools for exploring literacy. The maps are highly interactive and provocative, pushing learners to discern patterns and interactions in materials and concepts.

Thinking Maps are used in constructing knowledge and discerning the concepts that organize the expectancies and rules of phonics. Dorling [knowing] the sounds of the past tense, /t/, /d/, and /id/ can lead to the understanding that the sound of this morpheme is based upon the last sound in the root word to which it is affixed. Using the Brace Map, students identify these part-whole relationships. Finding the similarities and differences between syllable types using Double Bubble Maps leads to the understanding that each syllable is defined by its vowel. Creating a Flow Map for sequencing the spelling of /ch/, ch or tch, /j/, ge or dge, and /k/ k or ck, at the end of a word can lead to the concept that the spelling depends upon what type of vowel is in that word.

I use a "step card" strategy with learners for defining, organizing, and promoting self-monitoring and metacognition. A step card is a basic skill of sequencing using the Flow Map. A step card simply states the steps or thinking process as a physical Flow Map for solving a problem. Examples might include knowing how to read or spell a multisyllable word, knowing how to pronounce the letter C, being able to summarize a paragraph or paraphrase a passage, or following the steps of reciprocal learning when reading a passage. The step card includes questions as well as decision points. Each student creates a description of the process in his or her own words. Eventually students collect their own compendium of step cards for literacy, which becomes a resource for writing and reading experiences.

Thinking Maps also provide concrete tools for teachers as they make the direct link between phonemic awareness and reading comprehension strategies. During teacher training for the California Literacy Initiative, I asked middle school teachers to read a short story, "Salvador, Early and Late," by Sandra Cisneros. The directions were to read the passage, visualizing the images of Salvador and in small groups to cooperatively create a Bubble Map to describe the main character. The teachers also were to present their maps and their thinking-process to the entire class.

As the teachers worked, they naturally began to sort and categorize their thoughts and ideas, which lead to the creation of a Tree Map. Other teachers began seeing similarities and differences between Salvador's behavior at school and at home, creating the thought process for a Double Bubble Map. Others began to hypothesize why this main character felt and behaved as he did, a cause-and-effect pattern developed through the Multi-Flow Map. All of these thought patterns were mediated by questions, Thinking Maps, and guiding suggestions. This simple assignment became a meaningful, interactive process that engaged and enhanced each participant's comprehension of the material. This Thinking Maps activity was the foundation for direct use of these tools by students and a bridge between phonemic awareness and metacognition.

Thinking Maps Software

The development of phonemic awareness overlaps with the growing capacity of students' reading comprehension abilities. Unlike the example above, the two are often on separate tracks. But, underlying the two is students' fundamental capacity to think in patterns. Reading is often facilitated in reading groups and through one-on-one instruction, but in the past 10 years a growing number of students have been learning to read with support from software programs. As these are not high-end artificial intelligence programs, it's not surprising that few actually provide a way for students to actively and consciously apply thinking patterns as text structures.

In the next example, a 1st grader uses Thinking Maps and Thinking Maps Software to collect, organize, and then write a book on a special topic. Thinking Maps Software is not a reading comprehension program, nor is it a "content"-specific program. Rather, it is a unique visual processor, with three windows: one for teacher questions to students, a second for students to create Thinking Maps, and a third window that is a basic word processor (Figure 6.6).

William Waste, a computer science teacher at Lebanon High School, in Lebanon, New Hampshire, has used Thinking Maps Software with his students. In Figure 6.7, he describes the capabilities of the software.

As stated above, "reading" the world is more than just reading text, and often a field trip is an experience that blends language and experience into a wealth of understanding for a young student. Here is a description of the process and the product by Terri Riley, parent of 1st grader Jackson Riley (Figures 6.8, 6.9, and 6.10 show Jackson's maps and drawings about monkeys).

A Field Trip

BY TERRI RILEY

Before a field trip to the North Carolina Zoo, Jackson was assigned an animal to observe and research. After carefully observing the animal at the zoo and reading books about it, he was asked to describe it and find out about its habitat, food, enemies, and some interesting facts. Because he had recently learned to use a Bubble Map and a Tree Map, it made perfect sense to use them for taking notes. Jackson would stop as he read to place appropriate information into each map. I was amazed how easily he completed the research. He was excited about using the Thinking Maps Software to make maps for his presentation at school. He became so captivated with his findings that he decided to write his own book using his maps.

This example shows how experiential learning, reading from texts, drawings, Thinking Maps and Software, and writing may be synthesized into a final product. While the field trip and reading alone provided a rich learning experience, the Thinking Maps supported the student to make sense of the experience by patterning the information. The maps also became part of a final product. These multiple ways of expressing information show a richness of information, motivate the reader to read on, and guide readers to a full comprehension of the information. For Jackson, this product gave much greater meaning to the experience of learning

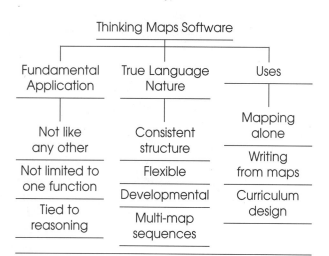

FIGURE 6.6

Thinking Maps Software Tree Map

FIGURE 6.7

Thinking Maps Software:
A Tool for Expanding Thinking
by William Waste

Just as word processors have been specifically designed to apply the capabilities of computers to written language and spreadsheet programs are designed for numbers or database applications for files of information, so has Thinking Maps Software (TMS) been created to facilitate the use of Thinking Maps as a visual language. Unlike other graphic applications, such as "draw" programs, TMS can help students apply Thinking Maps in an extensive number of ways from map creation for personal organization, to cooperative map-based communication, to the combination of both maps and writing. The software thus extends the basic strength of Thinking Maps by being grounded in the connection between specific visual patterns and discrete reasoning patterns.

By providing the structure to map building, TMS makes it far easier to create clear, effective maps, and to make changes to them just as a word processor has made it easier to create and then edit text. This also supports the developmental qualities of Thinking Maps. Effective map use can be seen by both preschool children and by adults, albeit with clear developmental differences in complexity and use.

The software also has a variety of ways it can be used to fit the needs of novice to expert users. If each Thinking Map represents an element of vocabulary in the visual language, then the ability to create multiple maps in sequence allows for the building of "visual sentences" that expand the power of the eight graphics into a true visual language for thinking. TMS greatly expands the ability of people to use Thinking Maps together and is bringing about new applications of the maps that have not been realized before. One of these areas is in the use of the maps by themselves as a form of communication. It is now much easier for teachers to write and share curriculum, and for students to quickly generate, save, swap and reconfigure maps and writing as the patterns are transmitted from classroom to classroom, across districts, and around the world.

Thinking Maps have established a new level of use for graphics, and the Thinking Maps Software builds upon these strengths and unique qualities, enabling learners to expand their thinking in ways that have been unimaginable until now.

about an animal. It also improved his capacity to seek, organize, and express information, just as students in Bob Fardy's 2nd grade classrooms were able to think through information about rocks and create a Rock Rubric using multiple Thinking Maps (discussed in Chapter 2).

Researching a Famous African American's Life

Unfortunately, *rarely* are students able to visit the sites that give them a hands-on experience. This is especially true in the area of history. Although the Internet, CD-ROM, and video mate-

FIGURE 6.8

A 1st Grader's Bubble Map About Monkeys

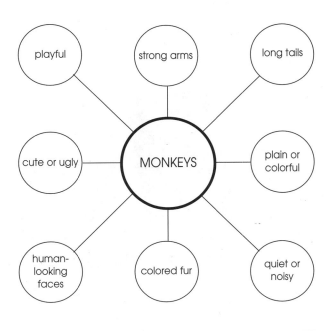

FIGURE 6.9

A 1st Grader's Drawings and Writings About Monkeys

Monkeys have strong arms and long tails. They have human-looking faces.

Monkeys like different kinds of foods. Some like nuts, leaves, and fruits. Other monkeys like birds' eggs and insects.

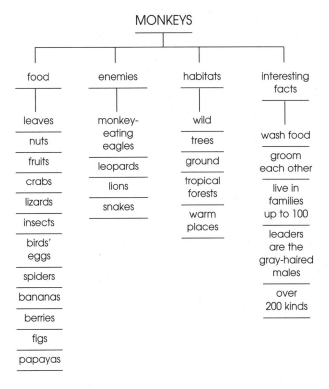

FIGURE 6.10

A 1st Grader's Tree Map on Monkeys

difficult for her students. But all teachers and students in this inner-city K–5 school had been trained for years in the use of Thinking Maps and had applied these tools across disciplines. By the time the 5th graders faced this objective, they had become fluent with all eight tools for patterning thinking in reading, writing, and mathematics. They had also learned how to use multiple maps together in order to create final products. Let's look at how one student independently used Thinking Maps to generate, organize, and sequence information before writing her essay about the life of Frederick Douglass.

First, the student used a Bubble Map to identify key attributes of Frederick Douglass (see Figure 6.11). This map is based on the cognitive skill

FIGURE 6.11

A 5th Grader's Bubble Map on Frederick Douglass

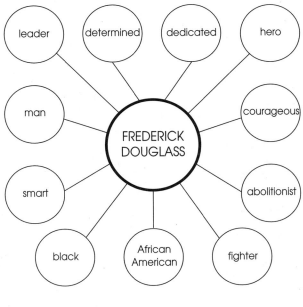

rial are providing a richer resource than history textbooks, most of the learning in classroom is text based. The "cognitive load" required by students to sustain a lengthy research project using texts is daunting. For example, consider this learning objective presented by a New York City 5th grade teacher to her class: *In celebration of Black History Month, research and write a report on a famous African American.*

This teacher knew that the first attempt at a multi-step research process was going to be of identifying attributes of things and developing a descriptive cluster of qualities of the man: dedicated, smart, courageous, determined, and so on. She then used a Tree Map for categorizing, or sorting the information into the paper topic, the supporting ideas, and a detailed factual record (see Figure 6.12). The Tree Map helped her synthesize a vast quantity and varying qualities of ideas while deleting extraneous details. Last, to create a logical progression of ideas for writing, she used the Flow Map (Figure 6.13). The outcome from these Thinking Maps was a highly scored 10-paragraph essay that mirrored the Flow Map you see. Additionally, the student submitted the three maps in typed form, providing evidence of the thinking process she used on the way to the final product.

Let's look back at the three types of visual tools and the clusters of behaviors related to this student's work in order to see how Thinking Maps act as a synthesis of these other kinds of visual tools for facilitating intelligent behaviors.

First, much as when using *brainstorming webs*, which support creative and flexible thinking, this student was able to investigate Frederick Douglass starting with blank pages, developing map after map of ideas drawn from resources available in the school. She was able to link information from map to map as well, thus easily *transforming* information into different patterns of thought. While the Bubble Map is specifically used for identifying attributes or characteristics, it gave the student a way to abstract from linear textual sources the essential qualities of Douglass into a rich cluster of information.

Second, much as with the use of *graphic organizers*, this student shows that the starting points—or common graphic primitives—for each Thinking Map effectively facilitate perseverance in the task. The student was able to stay focused on the lengthy, multi-step requirements of the project: collection of research, organization, and, finally, production of a piece of writing. The design of the Tree Map and Flow Map gave support to this kind of systematic integration of knowledge. She could create a hierarchy of ideas using the Tree Map and a sequence for paragraph structure using the Flow Map. These two tools also supported the precise relating of information.

Third, as with other *thinking-process maps*, it is clear that this student had become aware of

FIGURE 6.12

A 5th Grader's Tree Map on Frederick Douglass

Frederick Douglass's Life

Obstacles He Had to Overcome
1. Slavery
2. Never seeing his mom when he was little
3. Never knowing his father
4. Being beaten and whipped
5. Having a law that makes him not able to learn to read and write
6. Not having enough clothes to wear, or enough food
7. Being hunted by the slave catchers after he escaped

Major Accomplishments
1. Escaped to freedom
2. Learned to read and write
3. Wrote articles and books
4. American consul to Haiti

Things That Frederick Did to End Slavery
1. Made speeches
2. Wrote books
3. Helped get people to fight against the south in the Civil War
4. Talked to people

FIGURE 6.13

A 5th Grader's Flow Map on Frederick Douglass

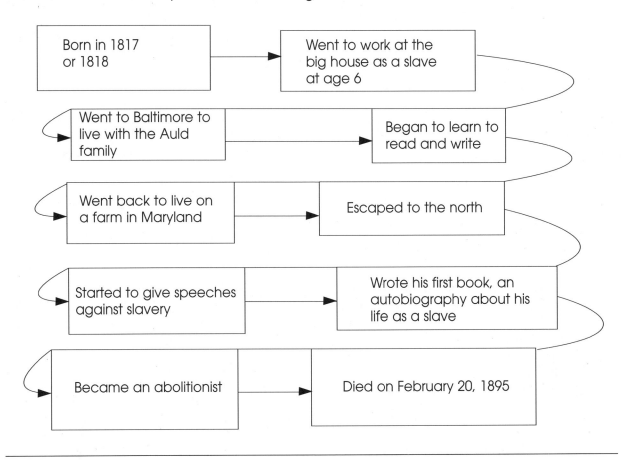

the multiple cognitive tools necessary for completing the task. While she may have had guidance from the teacher along the way, this student's fluency with the tools enabled her to configure the Thinking Maps to her evolving understandings about Frederick Douglass. She was able to chunk the information and consciously form the information into different cognitive patterns that enabled her to write the essay. Most students are unable to do these tasks, especially when confronted with the otherwise daunting learning objective of first researching, then organizing, and finally writing an essay report.

Lesson Planning and Essential Questions

As discussed, the eight Thinking Maps are used together much as a carpenter uses a tool kit: individual and multiple maps may be used in very flexible configurations in order to construct patterns and make meaningful networks of knowledge. More important to classroom practice, as we shall see, an essential question is embedded in each visual tool.

Deborah Meier, along with colleagues and students at Central Park East Elementary and Secondary Schools in New York City, developed a few essential questions that became central to their curriculum design and classroom interactions:

> The question of evidence, or "How do we know what we know?"; the question of viewpoint in all its multiplicity, or "Who's speaking?"; the search for connections and patterns, or "What causes what?" supposition, or "How might things have been different?"; and finally, why any of it matters, or "Who cares?" (Meier, 1995, p. 50)

These questions are based in fundamental ways of seeing the world from different perspectives, requiring students to seek patterns and connections *within* multiple frames of reference. Like the questions above, each Thinking Map—along with the "frame" of reference around each map—represents a reflective question:

1. Circle Map: What are the context and frame of reference?

2. Bubble Map: What are the attributes?

3. Double-Bubble Map: How are these alike and different?

4. Tree Map: How are these grouped together?

5. Brace Map: What are the parts of the whole?

6. Flow Map: What was the sequence of events?

7. Multi-Flow Map: What were the causes and effects?

8. Bridge Map: Is there an analogy between these ideas?

By linking concrete maps with essential questions and abstract thought processes, students can deal with more complex thinking because they know *what it looks like*. Importantly, they come to know how to link multiple Thinking Maps together in response to the *multiple* essential questions that teachers ask most every day.

A clear example is found at St. George's School in Wanganui, New Zealand. Over the past few years, the whole school has become fluent with the essential questions and dynamic graphics of Thinking Maps. St. George's has integrated Thinking Maps into its ongoing development with Art Costa's intelligent behaviors, rubric development, learning styles, action learning, and a high-tech school environment. With the entry of Thinking Maps into this rich array of practices, curriculum design and essential questions are often linked to Thinking Maps.

One example of this ease of integration is a lesson plan designed for students at the middle school level for investigating two explorers (see Figure 6.14). Students are fluent with the Thinking Maps, so as you can see, they are not even given questions—only the requirement to *show their thinking* using the maps, write an evaluation, and present the maps to the classroom.

This mental fluency with the Thinking Maps by all administrators, teachers, and students in the school led several teams of teachers to create a rubric for using Thinking Maps (see Figure 6.15).

Professional portfolios developed by many teachers on using Thinking Maps in the school also show the developmental aspects of the maps across grade levels and content areas.

Alan Cooper, former principal of the school, describes the background on how this rubric was developed. This rubric and Cooper's writing reveal the power of the development of rubrics by a school faculty and the depth to which this rubric shows the effectiveness of Thinking Maps.

FIGURE 6.14

A Middle School-Level Social Studies Activity: Thinking Maps and Explorers

SOCIAL STUDIES TOPIC   (Term 4, Weeks 1–4)
Two Famous Explorers with a Focus on Thinking Maps

- We will study people distant in time and space by reading and studying two contrasting explorers.
- Our context for study will be: "When confronted with difficulties . . ."
- We will study such contexts as
  - Tolerance
  - Aspirations
  - Conflict
  - Control
  - Influence
  - Participation
  - Respecting
  - Success
  - Courage
  - Endurance

You will need to choose your two explorers and the appropriate Thinking Map to
  - Define them in context
  - Classify and organize your information
  - Compare and contrast your two explorers using descriptives
  - Show cause and effect of each exploration
  - Show the sequences of steps leading to the highest achievement of each of your explorers
  - Show the environment that your explorers experienced in wholes and parts
  - See analogies using explorers in general and the environment that they have explored (or achievement)

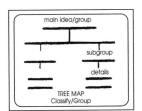

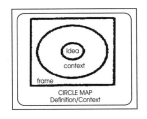

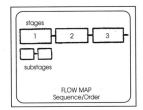

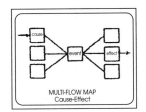

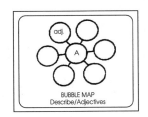

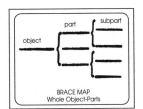

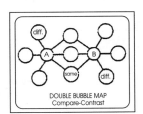

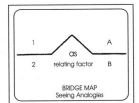

—Used with the permission of Alan Cooper, Gill Corballis, and Georgette Jensen, St. George's School.

FIGURE 6.15

Rubric for Using Thinking Maps

	Teacher Responsible	Learning Community	Outcome
NOVICE	1. Attend inservice courses. 2. Observe classroom. 3. Put standardized maps on the wall. 4. Read the Manual. 5. Introduce each Thinking Map to the Learning Community.	1. Children introduced to each Thinking Map separately. 2. Children are given specific maps for related work. 3. Students can recall names of each Thinking Map. 4. Children present work on standardized Thinking Maps.	1. Introduction of concepts of Thinking Maps by expert (a) to staff and (b) to students. 2. "Tools for Learning" Manual distributed to each class.
APPRENTICE	1. Model Thinking Maps in various contexts of a curriculum area. 2. Conduct class and group discussions on thinking processes of each map.	1. Children are demonstrating an awareness of which map to use. 2. Children are beginning to distinguish and use relevant maps. 3. Children are beginning to understand and define processes of Thinking Maps.	1. Use more than one Thinking Map regularly in one area of the curriculum. 2. Beginning to grasp concepts, processes, and definitions for each Thinking Map.
PRACTITIONER	1. Incorporate Thinking Maps into set work rather than using them in isolation. 2. Apply Thinking Maps to classroom activities (e.g., cooperative learning, routines). 3. Explore different ways of using Thinking Maps. 4. Display maps on walls and in books covering all subject areas.	1. Children are using Thinking Maps in many subject areas without prompting. 2. Children can justify the thinking processes in discussions. 3. Children are transferring Thinking Maps to content learning. 4. Thinking Maps are more detailed and creative. 5. Maps are revisited and added to, or edited, as tasks are worked through.	1. Use Thinking Maps regularly in many subject areas. 2. Ownership of Thinking Maps as tools for transferring thoughts, ideas, and information to content learning. 3. Explain how Thinking Maps help as tools for learning.
EXPERT	1. Team work: Mentor to Novice. 2. Take demonstration lessons with staff and students. 3. Raise to the conscious level of the student the thinking processes that are taking place. 4. Display versatility with Thinking Maps (e.g., use maps in reverse). 5. Encourage expanded thinking (e.g., idea formation). 6. Continually assess progress of students' thinking processes and abilities through metacognition and portfolios.	1. Students are integrating Thinking Maps into all classroom activities (e.g., curriculum, classroom routines, daily/weekly outlines). 2. Students are becoming mentors to other students. 3. Students use more than one type of Thinking Map for multi-step problems and/or content learning. 4. Students are diversifying Thinking Maps yet still keeping to thinking processes and concepts. 5. Students are able to assess their own thinking processes through metacognition.	1. Use all Thinking Maps consistently over all subject areas. 2. Integration of Thinking Maps into other areas of Innovative Learning such as Learning Styles and Intelligent Behaviors.

—Used with the permission of Alan Cooper, Gill Corballis, and Georgette Jensen, St. George's School.

Thinking Maps Rubric

BY ALAN COOPER

Successful teachers are craftsmen and crafts-women. Not only do they have the necessary skills for the teaching required of them, but they also have a passionate pride in what they are doing that transcends the meaning of the job. They achieve this by familiarizing themselves thoroughly with what they are doing so that they become positive models, set standards, and are practical in what they do, along with artistic, aesthetic input as well. This has happened with Thinking Maps.

Familiarization with the Tools. Familiarization requires practical usage. It will happen quicker if all aspects of the school culture embrace it. For teachers and myself, this means using Thinking Maps in teacher plans, both long and short term; in the routine notices about the classroom walls and the corridors of the school; and in the actual teaching. In other words, Thinking Maps need to become an important part of the school culture. Both peer, administrative, and parent support may be needed, as tension will be engendered—as always occurs—when the old paradigm is replaced or significantly added to. A side effect is that teachers may well have a new empathy for students, as they too struggle to learn how to apply the new language of Thinking Maps deeply.

Thinking Maps Rubric for Standards. Rubrics are a very satisfactory way of setting standards. While it is somewhat innovative to set rubrics for teacher growth, it is also logical. We have done this with Thinking Maps. The notion of integrity at least suggests that if rubrics aid the growth of students, then they will also aid the growth of teachers. In our rubrics teachers have a clear progression from the novice to the expert model. In addition, we have constructed a rubric for the learning community. Thus, on the one

hand, we are aiding the individual teacher's professional development using Thinking Maps, while on the other we are ensuring that our efforts fit within the vision of the school and are not simply an add-on, which in the past teacher professional development has often been.

Perhaps a little more explanation is necessary. Even where whole school development is undertaken, individual teachers frequently are concerned only with the progress that they are making with their students. But Thinking Maps facilitate long-term development of students' thinking over multiple years. The idea behind the second column of the rubric (Figure 6.15) is a whole school overview so that the parts (teachers' and students' progress) are integrated into the whole (the school). This effect could easily translate beyond the school to the district. Portfolios can become very important artifacts here, especially so when the teacher's reflection and meta-cognition are integrated with those of the student, a mentor, and supervisors.

Interpreting Texts over Time: Shakespeare

Fifteen years ago, I had the opportunity to teach *Romeo and Juliet* to an 11th grade "remedial reading" class at McClymonds High School in the inner-city of Oakland, California. There were not enough copies of the play for every student, the students' reading level averaged from the 4th to the 6th grade, and they had never heard of an author by the name of Shakespeare. To say the least, the text as it stood was way outside of their context, but the story and themes were not. After I read Act 1 out loud for the class—with many starts and stops—and asked some basic comprehension questions, I realized that they could not follow the plot and were not able to recall the confusion of characters, antiquated language, and shifting settings. Somehow I needed to support them in seeing the evolving story line.

After a week of frustration, I brought in butcher paper and wrapped the inside walls of the room much like the artist Cristo wrapping the outside of a building in colored ribbons. We reviewed Act 1 by making a Flow Map, chunking the sequence of events, and introducing key characters and family relationships. By the end of the play we had butcher paper flowing around the room, visibly wrapped around our minds. I could then ask interpretive questions, students could access the essential events of the whole play in the turn of a head. While we did not get to the level of analysis I expected, these students, maybe for the first time, had mapped out a whole story. They had a tool for making sense of any text and saw that the interpretive process requires the patterning of a story's pieces. Without this Flow Map, these students could not have held the whole play in their minds and been able to abstract themes—which they realized reached into their own lives—from across this romance.

Some years later, after introducing the eight Thinking Maps to a group of teachers, I received a unit of study created by a 9th grade student in Los Angeles who was required to use Thinking Maps as note-making tools for comprehending *Julius Caesar*. While the space is not available for all 12 maps created by this student, his reflections on the process reveal not only the initial response to these tools, but his immediate transfer of the tools across the high school, and his vision of future possibilities (see Figure 6.16).

Adult Literacy

The visual tools and language of Thinking Maps presented above provide a new avenue for students and teachers. In the examples we may see

> **A 9th Grader's Metacognitive Statement**
>
> **Making these Thinking Maps has helped my understanding of Julius Caesar immensely. Before I completed the maps, I understood the basic concepts and context of the play, but if I were given a test on it I wouldn't have done very well. I have an outline in my head and a better comprehension of the important characters of the play. . . .**
>
> **At first I thought these maps were just busywork. . . . [But] the maps have helped me to study and to learn the materials. They help us to organize our thoughts and improve the comprehension of anything we read.**

that students can develop their capacities to be creative and flexible, to persevere and to be systematic, and to be reflective and self-aware of cognitive patterns to the degree that they can readily apply these patterns to challenging performance. Yet, we also now know that like our brains, our students must continue to grow and adapt over their lifespans.

At Jones Junior College, in Laurel Mississippi, Dr. Marjann Ball has used Thinking Maps for several years with her adult learners, many of whom are returning to school to advance their life skills and step into new professions. Many students

FIGURE 6.16

A 9th Grader's Double Bubble Map on Julius Caesar

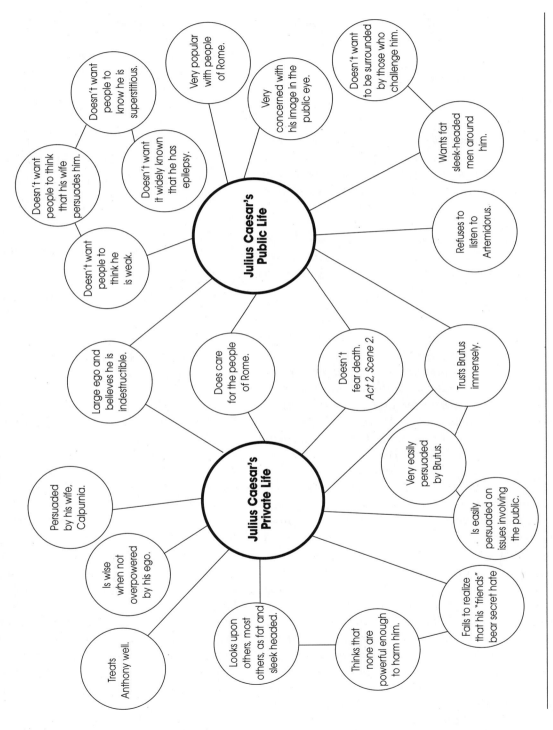

Julius Caesar's Public Life

- Doesn't want people to know he is superstitious.
- Very popular with people of Rome.
- Very concerned with his image in the public eye.
- Doesn't want to be surrounded by those who challenge him.
- Doesn't want people to think that his wife persuades him.
- Doesn't want it widely known that he has epilepsy.
- Wants fat sleek-headed men around him.
- Doesn't want people to think he is weak.
- Refuses to listen to Artemidorus.

Shared:
- Large ego and believes he is indestructible.
- Does care for the people of Rome.
- Doesn't fear death. *Act 2, Scene 2.*
- Trusts Brutus immensely.

Julius Caesar's Private Life

- Persuaded by his wife, Calpurnia.
- Is wise when not overpowered by his ego.
- Treats Anthony well.
- Looks upon others, most others, as fat and sleek headed.
- Thinks that none are powerful enough to harm him.
- Fails to realize that his "friends" bear secret hate.
- Very easily persuaded by Brutus.
- Is easily persuaded on issues involving the public.

enter Marjann's reading class barely able to read. Here is her story:

Reading in Junior College

BY MARJANN BALL

As an instructor of reading, study skills, and English for the past 19 years in a junior college, I have seen many students confront difficulties in processing information. Their variances in reading abilities from the 4th grade upward, as well as in their range in ACT scores, have added to the complexity of the problem. In spite of the disparity in abilities, a commonality exists between the students who can read well and those who cannot: very few possess the thinking strategies necessary to process what they read.

Some years back I tried various thinking skills approaches, but I discovered that there was very little transfer to reading across disciplines. Since I began using Thinking Maps seven years ago, my observations, testimonials from students, and my doctoral research have confirmed that my search for a vehicle to transfer and integrate thinking skills in all areas is over. My research confirmed what my experience showed: a highly significant correlation between the use of Thinking Maps and improved reading comprehension scores of my students (Ball, 1999). [See Appendix B, p. 137, for information about her lesson plan.]

Students who learn to use Thinking Maps in my reading and study skills course continually bring in examples of their applications. One nontraditional student, returning to college after 20 years in the workforce, was failing economics. He began using the maps to organize the voluminous material and, by the end of the semester, had made an A. A "traditional" nursing student was having difficulty remembering details in an anatomy course. After using the Thinking Maps and Software to organize the information, her scores on tests increased as well as her retention of the information later in the year.

At the end of every semester I have students evaluate the course and identify the most helpful strategies they learned. Over the past three years (nine classes), between 85 to 90 percent of the students identified Thinking Maps as the most helpful tools for learning and transfer across their other classes.

Some of my students also elaborated with comments about the Thinking Maps, such as:

- *"Thinking Maps are the best strategy I have ever used to organize and help me recall information."*
- *"The Thinking Maps allow me to see what I'm thinking and then reflect on what I thought."*
- *"Why didn't we learn these in elementary school? Or on the job?"*
- *"May I take these home to my children?"*

A Dynamic Language of Visual Tools

As you visually scan this chapter, from applications for phonemic awareness in kindergarten to advanced work in college-level courses, it becomes clear that Thinking Maps is a dynamic language that may be flexibly used from early childhood to late in life. This is evident in the above quote: a parent in a junior college course wanting to take these tools home to use with her children.

The structure and theory of this visual language is based on eight fundamental cognitive skills that human beings use and improve upon *lifelong*. The maps provide a dynamic visual representation and graphic starting point for applying these skills as patterns of thinking. The dynamism and developmental capacity of Thinking Maps reveals that, unlike mostly singular visual tools reviewed in this book, students learn to independently and cooperatively apply these eight maps as interdependent patterns for transforming information into knowledge and products of thinking.

The teachers, parents, administrators, and students who have used these tools see direct benefits in content-specific learning and processes that are standardized and tested, but something more is evident. All learners are improving their thinking in a very conscious way *over time* as they use this language year after year in whole schools. This common visual language is not only challenging assumptions about abilities to think, but also is giving learners the practical tools for shifting these mind-sets from seeing deficits to seeing the power of the human brain and mind to seek and create meaningful patterns in different contexts.

Openness is composed of two basic parts. The first depicts a high plateau, wild and barren. It implies emptiness. The second part originally symbolized two humans standing back to back on a mound, a vantage point from which they could see in all directions. (Lao-tzu, 1986 trans. by R. L. Wing)

Drawing by K. P. Lau.

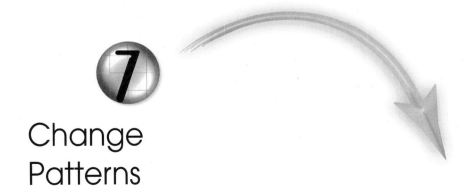

7

Change
Patterns

Changing Minds

*New frameworks are like climbing mountains—
the larger view encompasses, rather than rejects,
the earlier more restricted view.*

—Albert Einstein

This *Field Guide* is fundamentally about change and how visual tools facilitate change at many levels and over a lifespan of learning. What is *change*? On the most basic level, change is the process of transforming something, not into something completely new, but encompassing the old and bringing it into a new *form*. New forms are *physically* integrated into new neural networks in the brain, changing the mind, and possibly changing the outward behaviors of a learner.

The power inherent in most visual tools is the capacity to support individual learners in transforming what otherwise would be perceived as strictly linear experiences, text and data, into a more expressive visual pattern—sometimes linear and other times nonlinear—that more deeply reflects the holism of the concept. When a stu-

dent drafts a visual expression, he or she is forming the static information into knowledge, much as a sculptor transforms a dead block of clay into a life-full image. So often we give students lifeless blocks of clay in classrooms, and they turn them back to us *in the same form.*

An exemplar of transformative visual tools—which *every* student could immediately use and gain from—is found in the History Alive! program (Teachers' Curriculum Institute, 1994). Although this program brings history to students through activities and discovery units that employ multiple intelligences, students synthesize their work using a range of visual tools. They create Interactive Student Notebooks (see Figure 7.1). On facing pages in students' notebooks, the right page consists of teacher-directed input, which may include handouts, linear notes, and outlines. On the left side, students transform the information provided into a full range of visual tools shown in this book, and other representations of their thinking. This explicit focus—seeing with two eyes—creates a dynamic environment in the classroom for honoring both what the teacher is

FIGURE 7.1

Left Side/Right Side: A Student's Interactive Notebook

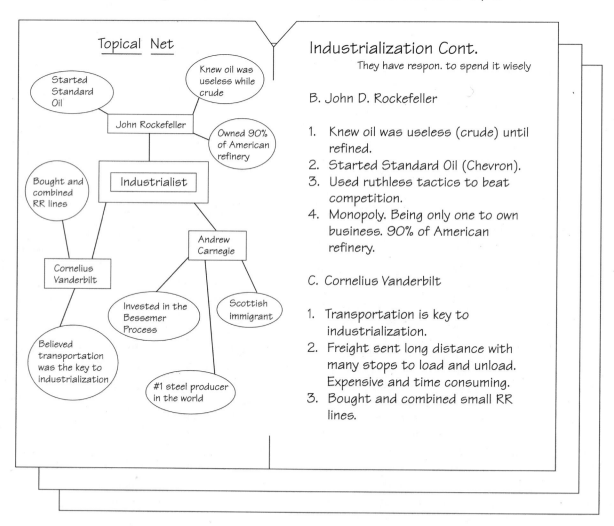

Left Side
Student Processing "Output"

Right Side
Teacher-Directed "Input"

Topical Net

Started Standard Oil

Knew oil was useless while crude

John Rockefeller

Owned 90% of American refinery

Bought and combined RR lines

Industrialist

Andrew Carnegie

Cornelius Vanderbilt

Invested in the Bessemer Process

Scottish immigrant

Believed transportation was the key to industrialization

#1 steel producer in the world

Industrialization Cont.

They have respon. to spend it wisely

B. John D. Rockefeller

1. Knew oil was useless (crude) until refined.
2. Started Standard Oil (Chevron).
3. Used ruthless tactics to beat competition.
4. Monopoly. Being only one to own business. 90% of American refinery.

C. Cornelius Vanderbilt

1. Transportation is key to industrialization.
2. Freight sent long distance with many stops to load and unload. Expensive and time consuming.
3. Bought and combined small RR lines.

Source: Teachers' Curriculum Institute. (1994). *History alive! Interactive student notebook.* Mountain View, CA: Teachers' Curriculum Institute. Copyright © 1994 by Teachers' Curriculum Institute. Reprinted with permission.

presenting and the expectation that students will transform this new information into a new form.

By being able to step back from a visual representation and see "the larger view," learners and teachers can make richer inferences, interpretations, and understandings. The "more restricted view" may be held in the lines of linear text and spoken language. When using a creative web, an organizer, or a map, a student is in the process of changing the actual form of the information, transforming and constructing the information into knowledge by his or her hand.

This split perspective opens a classroom to multiple perspectives. Unlike any other period in the history of humankind, learners of today must be able to see that as they are looking down on their maps, they are looking at only one perspective, one mental model. In the culturally diverse, information-rich, high-end communication world, students must see that mental models are

> like a pane of glass framing and subtly distorting our vision; mental models determine what we see.
> Human beings cannot navigate through the complex environments of our world without these cognitive mental maps, and all these maps, by definition, are flawed in some way. (Senge, Kleiner, Roberts, Ross, & Smith, 1994)

Without this critical perspective on mental models—and an understanding of the beliefs, values, and assumptions that frame mental models—visual tools for mapping our ideas will merely become another set of worthy tools for the teacher or student toolkit, rather than transformational tools for learners for reflecting on the processes of change.

Changing Organizations

As educators—and organizational leaders—we now understand that the individual learning is intimately tied to organizational learning. What is change in an organization? Cooperative learning in classrooms and collaborative working teams in the business world now are the norm rather than aberrant behavior. Change within these new parameters now relies on every level of the organization rather than only the top decision maker of the hierarchical organization. And, much like the mental models of the individual, group norms or mind-sets, theories-in-use, or schemata drive thinking and decision making in organizations:

Organization members frequently negotiate

> specifically *organizational* schemata. Such negotiations allow participants to have a common orientation toward events. Organizational schemata, therefore, generate shared meanings or frames of reference for the organization as a whole or for various subgroups within it. (Bartunek & Moch, 1987, p. 486)

A similar requirement of visual tools as change tools for the individual applies to organizational change. While this book is primarily about learners in classrooms, change in whole school communities (including students, parents, teachers, administrators, school board members, business community, and community leaders) now depends upon a sharing of the common and unique patterns of thinking of the members.

Unfortunately, in classrooms, whole schools, and in businesses, change is often a mere reinforcement of present patterns. As Bartunek and Moch describe it, this is *first-order change* (see box on p. 128). Sometimes change agents work with a faculty to facilitate the actors in identifying the mental models that are influencing their actions. They also help identify the existing decision-making process that drives change, and their mental models for perceiving assessment or "change processes" in their classrooms and across their school. This is all *second-order change*, as participants may make shifts in perception and behaviors according to these realizations.

Rarely, though, does an organization such as a school faculty become fluent enough with the processes of second-order change to be able to surface their own mental models—on their own—and actively evaluate and transform these understandings into new models for actions. This would-be *third-order change:* a conscious

---

Orders of Change

First-order change: **the tacit reinforcement of present understandings.**

Second-order change: **the conscious modification of present schemata in a particular direction.**

Third-order change: **the training of organizational members to be aware of their present schemata and thereby more able to change these schemata as they see fit.**

(Bartunek & Moch, 1987, p. 486)

---

and continuous process of expressing and transforming patterns of thinking and behaviors. (For a recent analysis of orders of change, transitions between orders, and implications for schools, see Zimmerman, 1999.)

I believe that even though we do not yet have the concrete "change tools" and processes to adequately engage in third-order change, this is exactly the direction we must go toward. I also believe that the visual expression of mental

models will be a key ingredient in this process. Why? Given a deeper understanding of visual tools as explicit ways to surface mental models, these maps become holistic forms for members to show the patterns and thus holism of their ideas (schemata) of learning communities to make change on their own.

Schoolwide Change

This *Field Guide* could have started with the following story of a school that is in the process of becoming part of a larger community of learners through the support of visual tools. Change is hard, and this school has certainly struggled with the same demons that confront every school: forces within and outside the school who, for whatever reason, resist change. Jeffrey Spiegel, the school's principal, offers this vision of his school, a school reflecting on its own process.

On Becoming A Metacognitive School

BY JEFFREY M. SPIEGEL

The Greek have a word, metanoic, *which when translated means fundamental shift of mind. At Hanover Street School (HSS), an elementary school in Lebanon, New Hampshire, students and teachers are considering news ways to think about thinking and integrate their discoveries into how teachers teach and students learn.*

At first blush HSS looks like an ordinary public school. Students gather on the playground prior to the school day to converse, play on the new climbing structure, and see who can reach the greatest heights on the swings. Like most schools, the hallways offer a glimpse of HSS's past and present. What distinguishes this school from others becomes apparent only when closely exam-

ining some unusual representations of student work, which are also prominently displayed in classrooms and corridors.

Students are representing their cognitive strategies with visual tools called **Thinking Maps.** It is the school's way of practicing metacognition, a principle of learning that exists when children are able to describe the thinking processes they use to solve problems. In Teaching With the Brain in Mind (1998b), Eric Jensen suggests that explicit learning models should include rich graphic organizers because they can provide an informational context for greater understanding and meaning.

One surprising consequence of Thinking Maps implementation was that teachers began discussing with students how to think about thinking. This dialogue represented the school's initial step to a new level of understanding about the learning and teaching process. Unbeknownst to many teachers, when students began describing strategies they used with Thinking Maps, they were embarking on a journey toward metacognitive development.

One display that captures visitors' attention in the 5th grade wing of the school is a rather large drawing (six feet long) by the class done with various color markers on blue construction paper. The title says "War," and below students created a giant Tree Map with branches that listed such categories as Causes, Results, Types of Warfare, Locations, and Weapons. Some subtopics were Transportation, Shelters, and Groups of People. As many as 30 examples appeared under each category.

In a 3rd grade classroom a depiction of bubbles emanates from a central circle with the words My Community inside. In the outer circles of the Bubble Map, students describe the local hospital, library, recreation center, and a host of other neighborhood resources and establishments.

These Thinking Maps demonstrate some of the many ways in which children in different grades and responding to various subject matter were able to organize information and visually represent it to others. Thinking Maps are not only an effective tool for classifying information and identifying problem-solving strategies. Additionally, they are effective communication and assessment tools that depict how children think and make sense about what they are learning.

Thinking Maps represent the common visual language teachers and students have been using to generate and organize ideas, to reflect on sequences of events, to characterize and contrast story elements, as well as to identify causes and effects of such varied topics as science reactions, pollution, slavery, or even discipline infractions. Students have created Brace Maps that describe physical parts of Aztec Shields, and Bridge Maps that show the relationship between book authors' styles and artists' techniques by way of analogies. This higher-order thinking by students represents a deeper understanding of curricular content that has surprised many teachers and parents.

The faculty at HSS now have a way to bridge curriculum with state-mandated outcomes commonly referred to as Frameworks. As in most states, the Frameworks identify curriculum standards and proficiencies for all subjects specific to each grade level. Students at HSS can display the thought processes they rely on to prepare writing prompts, solve multi-operational math problems, or describe relationships ranging from competing story protagonists to contrasting historical events that appear on the state Frameworks tests.

More impressively, Thinking Maps have provided new pathways for children to think at higher levels. Some students are becoming so adept with the maps, they no longer draw them. As one 6th grader remarked in a class meeting, "Instead of putting the map on paper to organize my thoughts, I can picture the map in my head and come up with the information right away."

Thinking Maps provide opportunities for students and teachers to talk about thinking and to work together to integrate their discoveries within the context of varied topics. Often, during the initial year of using them, students were able to create and apply innovative uses of the maps. This phenomenon was exciting and dynamic. It meant that students were not only in charge of their learning but that, in some classrooms, they were driving the instructional practice. This experience parallels Plato's concept of "educare" and the current movement focusing on the social nature of learning.

The use of Thinking Maps represents the cognitive side of metacognition. Students are now better able to describe their thinking strategies and apply them to traditional academic tasks.

Although Thinking Maps have been integrated into the curriculum, it is only the first step in HSS's efforts to create a metacognitive school. This past year the faculty and administration asked themselves, If Thinking Maps represent the cognitive side of metacognition, what then, constitutes the meta or experiential side? The answer: Community-Based Learning (CBL). CBL is composed of five primary organizational components: planning (assessment/essential questions), preparation (resonance with curriculum), action (implementation), reflection (evaluation), and recognition (social development). The Multi-Flow Thinking Map shown in Figure 7.2 describes some social causes required by academic standards and the effects of CBL on them that ultimately arrive at metacognitive learning. The map also provides a visual explanation of the relationships and interactive components that characterize a metacognitive school.

Understanding the Developmental Process

The Lebanon Food Coop Service Learning Project, initiated by 5th grade teacher, Sarah Curtis, represents one example of the professional growth process that characterized the integration of CBL and teacher development at HSS. Sarah responded

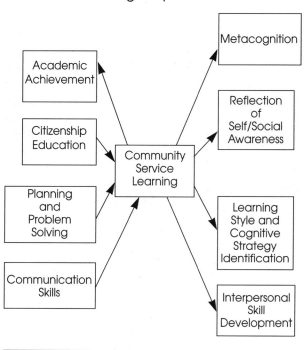

FIGURE 7.2

Multi-Flow Thinking Map

to the schoolwide effort to investigate, develop, implement, and evaluate the effectiveness of her class's CBL project as part of her staff development plan for the year.

The Food Coop Project resulted in the class's inquiry about the historical development of cooperatives dating back to the Rochdale Cooperative in early England. Students studied documents about the formation of the Lebanon Food Coop, and, based upon their research and discussions, performed a play written by Sarah at the cooperative's grand opening in the fall.

An analysis of the Food Coop Project, conducted by the New Hampshire State Study Group on Community Service Learning, revealed a number of significant findings. Consistent with other classroom first-time experiences with CBL, the Food Coop Project was teacher driven and lacked a formal reflection process for students. Furthermore, discussions with teachers revealed that they either did not know how or were initially reluctant to empower students in the planning process. While students spent many sessions exchanging ideas about their experiences, the process for student reflection in most cases was not formally defined. As a result, students focused more on what they learned personally from their CSL activity and less on describing the mental strategies they used to address a community-based issue.

Emerging from the Food Coop study was evidence that the teacher was adept at using Thinking Maps to assist the class in defining roles, organizing materials, and determining goals for the project. Students participated enthusiastically, applied academic skills, and gained historical, environmental and social perspectives about a business's responsibility to its community. Students also received positive recognition from local residents and, more important, influenced families to become Coop members. The play they preformed was filmed, and the video has now become a permanent fixture in the Coop's lending library.

The Lebanon Food Coop Project and other CBL class projects were innovative practices intended to broaden the context of learning for students, teachers, and community partners. Metacognitive schools create conscious, self-directed thinkers able to discover meaning through reflection and community experience. Thinking Maps and CBL experiences encourage students to reflect on their work critically and creatively so that learning becomes a deeper and more intimate process.

Metacognitive Teaching as a Developmental Process

CBL was not an entity separate from the conditions of learning and teaching at HSS. As the fac-

ulty discussed their CBL projects, they increasingly realized that this type of activity was a vehicle for learning how to plan instruction and how to think. Currently, the faculty is redefining the school's mission as a place for learning. It is what some in the literature have characterized as school development; namely "the process by which members of an institution develop the capacity to reflect on the nature and purpose of their work together" (Stewart, Prebble, & Duncan, 1997).

The initial experiences with Thinking Maps and CBL demonstrated that a developmental process described teachers' integration of new and provocative instructional practices. Based upon their experiences, teachers reconsidered the implications of the instructional planning process. In particular, they focused on the role assessment plays in unit study development.

Teachers began their discussions by considering their Thinking Maps experiences. Introduction and use of a new approach to teaching represented a developmental process of integration.

Teachers define assessment as the formative collection(s) of evidence(s) of learning. Assessment required a conscious plan to develop essential questions to guide the unit study and to determine what kind of student work would be assessed and with what formats (e.g., rubrics, formal tests, reports, projects, etc.). Assessment was distinguished from evaluation, which was defined as the analysis of the assessment evidence and the subsequent instructional reflection and planning with students that resulted.

Conclusion

Annually, HSS culminates the school year with a Celebration of Learning: an opportunity for the parents and local community to observe how HSS aspires to be a quality school. This year, for the first time, classes and community partners presented their CBL projects. It (1) represented a fundamen-

FIGURE 7.3

Maturing Outcomes Reflect Teachers' Growth

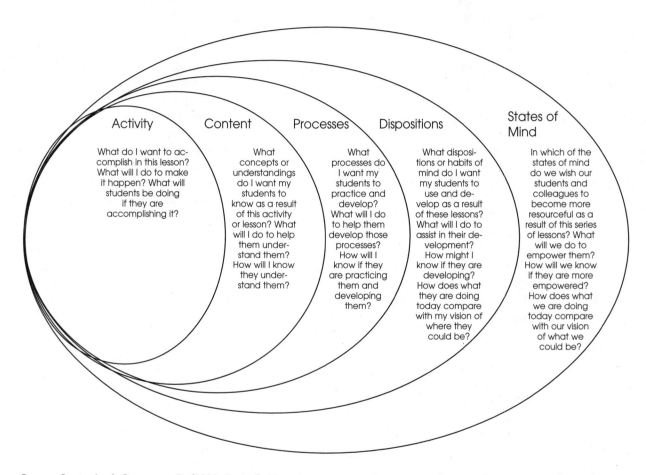

Activity

What do I want to accomplish in this lesson? What will I do to make it happen? What will students be doing if they are accomplishing it?

Content

What concepts or understandings do I want my students to know as a result of this activity or lesson? What will I do to help them understand them? How will I know they understand them?

Processes

What processes do I want my students to practice and develop? What will I do to help them develop those processes? How will I know if they are practicing them and developing them?

Dispositions

What dispositions or habits of mind do I want my students to use and develop as a result of these lessons? What will I do to assist in their development? How might I know if they are developing? How does what they are doing today compare with my vision of where they could be?

States of Mind

In which of the states of mind do we wish our students and colleagues to become more resourceful as a result of this series of lessons? What will we do to empower them? How will we know if they are more empowered? How does what we are doing today compare with our vision of what we could be?

Source: Costa, A., & Garmston, R. (1998, Spring). Maturing outcomes. *Encounter: Education for Meaning and Social Justice 11*(1), 11. Copyright © 1998 by Psychology Press. Reprinted with permission.

---

*tal or "metanoic" shift in how students are involved in the educational process, and (2) dramatized the first step by a school to encourage mutual learning through shared teaching by children and adults. As this powerful metacognitive environment slowly emerges and such programs as CBL and Thinking Maps are woven into the fabric of every classroom's educational program, HSS moves closer to becom-*ing a learning community that, no doubt, will have even greater cause for celebration.*

Shifting States of Mind

One way of looking at this *Field Guide* and the implications for change over time is through the lens developed by Art Costa and Robert Garmston (1998), with support from their colleagues. This model is one of maturing outcomes as a teacher grows over his or her career from reflecting on the outcomes of a specific activity, to seeing that the cumulative effect of activities are embedded in more comprehension, lifelong outcomes for learners (see Figure 7.3).

The activities we construct for students are embedded in layers of content and grown through natural processes. There are more inclusive and important questions that must ultimately frame and influence how these daily activities of content and process are formed. As Costa and Garmston ask: What are the habits and states of mind that we wish to develop in learners that will empower them to become aware of their own minds so that they can nimbly shift their own minds?

To do this, learners of all ages must be able to honestly reflect on their own thinking, to become aware of the patterns that seem to work, and to see how many patterns become lifeless, repetitive, unchanging, stubbornly unchangeable. Visual tools of all kinds provide pathways for learners—lifelong—to look inward, see, and then share with others how they are thinking. Thus, they can provide a visual pathway from where they are to a new vision of what could be.

Appendix A
Thinking Maps Test Scores Summary

This is a selected list of school results from several states around the country. All of the teachers in each of these schools and systems received comprehensive, cross-discipline training and classroom follow-up coaching for a minimum of one school year. The analysis and presentation of the test score results shown below were reported by administrators representing the schools or school systems in which the Thinking Maps were implemented. These results were submitted because they showed significant gains on the different test instruments used by the respective institutions. In all cases, the administrators have evidence that the results were directly related to the use of Thinking Maps by students. The scores are comparisons of results using state tests from year to year.

School/Description	Location	Test Instrument	Results
Margaret Fain Elementary/Title I (urban school)	Atlanta (Georgia) City Schools	Georgia State Test of Basic Skills	In 1996, reading scores rose from 29% to 69% in 1996; math scores rose from 32% to 63%.
Friendship Valley Elementary (suburban school)	Carroll County, Maryland	MSPAP (Maryland School Performance Assessment Program) State Performance Assessment	Scores rose across all six areas assessed with large gains in writing (27%), language (20.1%), and science (18.2%). Friendship Valley scores were second highest in the whole state in 1996 and have continued to grow in recent years.

School/Description	Location	Test Instrument	Results
Windemere Elementary (suburban school)	West Orange County, Florida	*Florida Writes!* State Assessment Stanford-8 Achievement Test	*Writing:* Significant rise in combined writing scores (from 2.7 to 3.4) on a 6-point scale. *Reading:* For two years scores were level at 68% and rose to 80% after implementation of Thinking Maps in 1997. *Math:* For two years scores were level at about 79% and rose to 92% after implementation.
Carl Waitz Elementary/100% Title I	Mission, Texas	Texas State: TAAS (Texas Assessment of Academic Skills)	*Reading:* Rose from 62.7% to 88.2% in 1994. *Math:* Rose from 41.2% to 76.5%.

Awards: Carl Waitz School was awarded a Texas Successful Schools excellence award for exceeding state standards, as well as a national Title I award for excellence. Waitz was also recognized by the Education Trust report as one of the few clear examples of minority and Title I students performing at high levels.

School/Description	Location	Test Instrument	Results
23 Catawba County Schools	North Carolina	North Carolina State End-of-Year Tests	

Results and Awards: All schools in Catawba County were trained in Thinking Maps from 1993–98. Below are results from several of the pilot schools that showed significant growth over multiple years. Fourteen schools received "exemplary" status from the state, and five of these received the "Schools of Distinction" status.

School/Description	Location	Test Instrument	Results
Claremont Elementary	Catawba County, North Carolina	North Carolina State End-of-Year Tests	*Writing:* From 1993–96, scores rose from 33% to 46% to 68% at the 4th grade level.

School/Description	Location	Test Instrument	Results
Tuttle Middle	Catawba County, North Carolina	North Carolina State End-of-Year Tests	*Writing:* From 1994–96, scores rose from 43.8% to 67.7% to 73% at the 8th grade level.
Chadbourne Elementary/Title I (rural)	Columbus County, North Carolina	North Carolina State End-of-Year Tests	*Writing:* From 1993–95, scores rose from 35.1% to 50.6% to 60.8%.

Award: Chadbourne received a National Title I Award as one of the top 100 Title I schools in the United States in 1995; students were performing well above both the county and state averages.

Morrisville Elementary (year-round)	Wake County, North Carolina, Research Triangle	North Carolina State End-of-Year Tests	*Writing:* A very high performing school; from 1993–96 scores rose from 32.5 to 69.4% to 76%.

Award: Morrisville was honored as one of *Redbook's* top 150 schools in the United States in 1995.

Brunswick County Schools/50% Title I	North Carolina	North Carolina State End-of-Year Tests	

Results: A comprehensive, countywide implementation of Thinking Maps began in 1996, grades K–12. Two years of test scores show that there was significant growth in reading, writing, and mathematics scores from 3rd–12th grades.

A. T. Allen Elementary	Cabarrus County, North Carolina	North Carolina State End-of-Year Tests	*Reading:* From 77% to 89% in 1998. *Writing:* From 29% to 77% in 1998. *Math:* 80% to 91% in 1998.

Source: Hyerle, D. (2000). *Thinking maps training of trainers resource manual,* vol. 1, pp. E-32, E-33. Raleigh, NC: Innovative Sciences, Inc. Copyright © 2000 by Innovative Sciences, Inc.

Appendix B
Reading Comprehension Using Thinking Maps
by Marjann Ball

Description of Treatment
Lesson Plan Using Thinking Maps Questions Sheet

During the 16-week semester, many reading skills were taught. For the purpose of this study, these reading skills were taught to both the experimental and control groups with the only difference being the use of Thinking Maps to teach and reinforce the reading skills in the experimental group.

For the first eight weeks of the semester, students in the experimental group were taught a reading concept using a Thinking Map and the control group was taught the same reading concept without the use of a Thinking Map. A short introduction of each Thinking Map was given at the beginning of each week with the reading concept for that week integrated into that Thinking Map. Only one Thinking Map was introduced per week with the sequence of maps being Circle, Bubble, Double Bubble, Tree, Brace, Flow, Multi-Flow, and Bridge.

After the first eight weeks of instruction in the experimental group, any Thinking Maps that were appropriate for the reading concept being taught were implemented. Thinking Maps were modeled by the instructor during lectures and used regularly by the students for homework assignments, projects, and assessments. Modeling, questioning, and reinforcing of the maps were essential as the students learned to use the tools.

The following plan was used:

Week	Control Group	Experimental Group
1	Building vocabulary. How words come into our culture.	Building vocabulary with Circle Map. How words come into our culture using Circle Map.
2 & 3	Context clues. Related words.	Context clues using Bubble Map. Related words using Double Bubble Map.
4	Figurative language.	Figurative language using Tree Map.
5	Parts of a textbook. SQ3R (Survey, Question, Read, Recall, Review) and PQRST (Preview, Question, Read, Self-Recite, Test (Review).	Parts of a textbook using Brace Map. SQ3R and PQRST using Brace Map.

Week	Control Group	Experimental Group
6	SQ3R and PQRST with textbook of choice.	SQ3R and PQRST with textbook using Flow Map.
7	Prediction and point of view.	Prediction and point of view using Multi-Flow Map.
8	Analogies.	Analogies using Bridge Map.
9	Test-taking strategies.	Test-taking strategies using Circle Map and Tree Map.
10	Analyzing through structure.	Analyzing through structure using Tree Map and Brace Map.
11	Main idea and supporting details.	Main idea and supporting details using Tree Map.
12	Critical reading: Fact and opinion.	Critical reading: Fact and opinion using Double Bubble Map.
13	Critical reading: Propaganda.	Critical reading: Propaganda using Tree Map and Multi-Flow Map.
14	Recreational reading.	Recreational reading with Thinking Maps.
15	Reading selections.	Reading selections with Thinking Maps.
16	Reading selections.	Reading selections with Thinking Maps.

Source: Ball, M. K. (1999). *The effects of thinking maps on reading scores of traditional and nontraditional college students.* Unpublished doctoral dissertation, University of Southern Mississippi, Hattiesburg. Used with permission.

Bibliography

Alcock, M. W. (1997, Spring). Are your students' brains comfortable in your classroom? *Ohio ASCD Journal* 5(2): 11–14.

Ambrose, S. E. (1996). *Undaunted courage: Meriwether Lewis, Thomas Jefferson, and the opening of the American West.* New York: Simon & Schuster.

Ausubel, D. P. (1968). *Educational psychology: A cognitive view.* New York: Holt, Rinehart, & Winston.

Ball, M. K. (1999). *The effects of thinking maps on reading scores of traditional and nontraditional college students.* Unpublished doctoral dissertation, University of Southern Mississippi, Hattiesburg.

Bartunek, J. M., & Moch, M. K. (1987). First-order, second-order, and third-order change and organizational development interventions: A cognitive approach. *The Journal of Applied Behavioral Science* 23(4): 483–500.

Belkin, L. (1998, August 23). Splice Einstein and Sammy Glick. Add a little Magellan. *New York Times Magazine*, sec. 6, p. 26, col. 1.

Bellanca, J. (1990). The cooperative think tank: Graphic organizers to teach thinking in the cooperative classroom. Arlington Heights, IL: SkyLight Publishing.

Bellanca, J. (1991). *Cooperative think tank, I and II.* Arlington Heights, IL: SkyLight Publishing.

Bromley, K., Irwin-De Vitis, L., & Modlo, M. (1995). *Graphic organizers.* New York: Scholastic.

Buckner, J. (1999). *Write from the beginning training manual.* Cary, NC: Innovative Sciences, Inc.

Buzan, T. (1979). *Use both sides of your brain.* New York: G. P. Dutton.

Buzan, T. (1996). *The mind map book.* New York: Plume/Penguin.

Caine, R. N., & Caine, G. (1994). *Making connections: Teaching and the human brain.* Menlo Park, CA: Addison-Wesley Pub. Co.

Capra, F. (1996). *The web of life: a new scientific understanding of living systems.* New York: Anchor Books.

Clarke, J. H. (1991). *Patterns of thinking.* Needham Heights; MA: Allyn and Bacon.

Costa, A. L., ed. (1991a). *Developing minds: A resource book for teaching thinking (rev. ed., Vols. 1 and 2).* Alexandria, VA: Association for Supervision and Curriculum Development.

Costa, A. L. (1991b). *The school as a home for the mind.* Palatine, IL: IRI/SkyLight Pub.

Costa, A., & Garmston, R. (1998, Spring). *Maturing outcomes. Encounter: Education for Meaning and Social Justice* 11(1): 11.

Costa, A. L., & Kallick, B., eds. (1995). *Assessment in the learning organization: Shifting the paradigm.* Alexandria, VA: Association for Supervision and Curriculum Development.

Csikszentmihalyi, M. (1991). *Flow.* New York: Harper Perennial.

Fanelli, S. (1995). *My map book.* New York: HarperCollins.

Fincher, S. (1991). *Creating mandalas*, p. 19. Boston: Shambhala.

Freire, P. (1970). *Pedagogy of the oppressed.* New York: Basic Books, Inc.

Gardner, H. (1983). *Frames of mind: The theory of multiple intelligences.* New York: Basic Books.

Gardner, H. (1985). *The mind's new science: A history of the cognitive revolution.* New York: Basic Books.

Gawith, G. (1987). *Information alive!* Auckland, NZ: Longman Paul Limited.

Gawith, G. (1996). *Learning alive!* Auckland, NZ: Longman Paul Limited.

Giamatti, A. B. (1980, July). The American teacher. *Harper's*, pp. 28–29.

Goleman, D. (1985). *Vital lies, simple truths: The psychology of self-deception.* New York: Touchstone.

Goleman, D. (1995). *Emotional intelligence.* New York: Bantam Books.

Grandin, T. (1996). *Thinking in pictures: And other reports from my life with autism.* New York: Vintage Books.

Horton, M., with Kohl, J., & Kohl, H. (1990). *The long haul: an autobiography.* New York: Doubleday.

Hughes, S. (1994). *The webbing way.* Winnipeg, Manitoba, Canada: Peguis Publishers Limited.

Hyerle, D. (1988–1993). *Expand your thinking* (Series: Pre-K–Grade 8). Cary, N.C.: Innovative Sciences, Inc.

Hyerle, D. (1990). *Designs for thinking connectively.* Lyme, N.H.: Designs for Thinking.

Hyerle, D. (1991). Expand your thinking. In A. L. Costa (Ed.), *Developing minds* (2nd ed.) (pp. 16–26). Alexandria, Va.: Association for Supervision and Curriculum Development.

Hyerle, D. (1993). "Thinking Maps as Tools for Multiple Modes of Understanding." Unpublished doctoral dissertation, University of California, Berkeley.

Hyerle, D. (1995). *Thinking maps: Tools for learning training manual.* Cary, NC: Innovative Sciences, Inc.

Hyerle, D. (December 1995/January 1996). Thinking maps: Seeing is understanding. *Educational Leadership 53*(4): 85–89.

Hyerle, D. (1996). *Visual tools for constructing knowledge.* Alexandria, VA: Association for Supervision and Curriculum Development.

Hyerle, D. (1999a). *Visual tools and technologies.* [Video]. Lyme, NH: Designs for Thinking.

Hyerle, D. (1999b). *Visual tools video and guide.* Lyme, NH: Designs for Thinking.

Hyerle, D. (2000a). *Thinking maps training of trainers resource manual.* Raleigh, NC: Innovative Sciences, Inc.

Hyerle, D. (2000b). Thinking maps: Visual tools for activating habits of mind. In A. L. Costa & B. Kallick (Eds.), *Activating and engaging habits of mind.* Alexandria, VA: Association for Supervision and Curriculum Development.

Hyerle, D. (Presenter). (2000c). *Visual tools: From graphic organizers to thinking maps* (elementary and secondary eds.). Sandy, UT: Video Journal of Education.

Hyerle, D., & Grey Matter Software. (1999). Thinking maps software. Cary, NC: Innovative Sciences, Inc.

Inspiration Software, Inc. (1998). *Classroom ideas using inspiration®.* Portland, OR: Inspiration Software, Inc.

Israel. L. (1991). *Brain power for kids.* Miami: Brain Power for Kids, Inc.

Jacobs, H. H. (1997). *Mapping the big picture: Integrating curriculum and assessment K-12.* Alexandria, VA: Association for Supervision and Curriculum Development.

Jago, C. (1995, December 27). Like drivers, schoolchildren require a clearly marked road map. *Los Angeles Times.*

Jensen, E. (1998a, August). Personal communication with author for publication in this book.

Jensen, E. (1998b). *Teaching with the brain in mind.* Alexandria, VA: Association for Supervision and Curriculum Development.

Jung, C. G. (1973). *Mandala symbolism.* Princeton, NJ: Princeton University Press.

Kallick, B. (1998). Personal communication with author for publication in this book.

Lakoff, G. (1987). *Women, fire, and dangerous things.* Chicago: University of Chicago Press.

Lakoff, G., & Johnson, M. (1980). *Metaphors we live by.* Chicago: University of Chicago Press.

Lakoff, G., & Johnson, M. (1999). *Philosophy in the flesh* (pp. 193–194). New York: Basic Books.

Lao-tzu. (1986). In *The Tao of power: A translation of the Tao te ching by Lao Tzu* (R. L. Wing, Trans.). Garden City, NY: Doubleday.

Lowery, L. (1991). The biological basis for thinking. A. L. Costa (Ed.) In *Developing minds: A resource book for teaching thinking, Vol. 1* (rev. ed.) (pp. 108–117). Alexandria, VA: Association for Supervision and Curriculum Development.

Margulies, N. (1991). *Mapping inner space.* Tucson, AZ.: Zephyr Press.

Marzano, R. J., Pickering, D., et al. (1997). *Dimensions of learning teachers' manual* (2nd ed.). Alexandria, VA: Association for Supervision and Curriculum Development.

McKenzie, J. (1998). Personal communication with author for publication in this book; and from: Graphical organizers. *FNO: From Now On: The Educational Technology Journal.* Web site: http://www.fno.org/.

Meier, D. (1995). *The power of their ideas: Lessons for America from a small school in Harlem.* Boston: Beacon Press.

Miller, G. A. (1956). The magical number seven, plus or minus two: Some limits on our capacity for processing information. *Psychological Review, 63,* 81–97.

Novak, J. D. (1998). *Learning, creating, and using knowledge: Concept maps as facilitative tools in schools and corporations.* Mahwah, NJ: Lawrence Erlbaum Associates.

Novak, J. D., & D. B. Gowin. (1984). *Learning how to learn.* Cambridge, England, and New York: Cambridge University Press.

Ogle, D. (1988, December/1989/January). Implementing strategic teaching. *Educational Leadership (46),* 47–48, 57–60.

Parks, S., & Black, H. (1992). *Organizing thinking, Book I.* Pacific Grove, CA: Critical Thinking Press and Software.

Richmond, B., S. Peterson, & P. Vescuso. (1998). STELLA. Hanover, NH: High Performance Systems.

Rico, G. L. (1983). *Writing the natural way.* Los Angeles: J. P. Tarcher, Inc.

Roth, W-M. (1994, January). Student views of collaborative concept mapping: An emancipatory research project. *Science and Education(78),* 1: 1–34.

Rowe, M. B. (1974). Wait time and rewards as instructional variables: Their influence on language, logic and fate control. *Journal of Research in Science Teaching* 11:81–94.

Secretary's Commission on Achieving Necessary Skills. (1991). *What work requires of schools: A SCANS report for America 2000.* Washington D.C.: U.S. Department of Labor.

Senge, P. M. (1990). *The fifth discipline.* New York: Currency Doubleday.

Senge, P., Kleiner, A., Roberts, C., Ross, R., & Smith, B. (1994). *The fifth discipline fieldbook: Strategies and tools for building a learning organization.* New York: Doubleday.

Shah, I. (1972). *Reflections,* p. 56. Baltimore: Penguin Books.

Shenk, D. (1997). *Data smog.* New York: HarperCollins.

Sinatra, R., & Pizzo, J. (1992, October). Mapping the road to reading comprehension. *Teaching K–8.*

Snyder, G. (1990). *The practice of the wild: Essays.* San Francisco: North Point Press.

Standing, L. (1973). *Quarterly Journal of Experimental Psychology, 25,* 207–222.

Stewart, D., Prebble, T., & Duncan, P. (1997). *The reflective principal.* Katonah, NY: Richard C. Owen Publisher.

Sylwester, R. (1995). A *celebration of neurons: An educator's guide to the human brain.* Alexandria, VA: Association for Supervision and Curriculum Development.

Teachers' Curriculum Institute. (1994). *History alive! Interactive student notebook.* Mountain View, CA: Teachers' Curriculum Institute.

Upton, A. (1960). *Design for thinking.* Palo Alto, CA: Pacific Books.

Wiggins, G., & McTighe, J. (1998). *Understanding by design.* Alexandria, VA: Association for Supervision and Curriculum Development.

Wolfe, P., & Sorgen, M. (1990). *Mind, memory, and learning.* Napa, CA: Authors.

Wolfe, P., & Sorgen, M. (1998, July). Personal communication with the author for publication in this book.

Wycoff, J., with Richardson, T. (1995). *Transformational thinking: Tools and techniques that open the door to powerful new thinking for every member of your organization.* New York: Berkley Books.

Zimmerman, D. P. (1998). *The role of reflexivity in the orders of change: The unraveling of the theories about second order change.* Unpublished doctoral dissertation. The Field Institute, Santa Barbara, California. (UMI Dissertation Services, Ann Arbor, Michigan).

Resources for Visual Tools

Books

Bromley, K., Irwin-De Vitis, L., & Modlo, M. (1995). *Graphic organizers*. New York: Scholastic.

Buzan, T. (1996). *The mind map book*. New York: Plume/Penguin.

Clarke, J. H. (1991). *Patterns of thinking*. Needham Heights, MA: Allyn and Bacon.

Hyerle, D. (1996). *Visual tools for constructing knowledge*. Alexandria, VA: Association for Supervision and Curriculum Development.

Moline, S. (1995). *I see what you mean*. York, ME: Stenhouse Press.

Videos

How to use graphic organizers to promote student thinking ["How To" Series, Tape 6]. (1999). Alexandria, VA: Association for Supervision and Curriculum Development.

Hyerle, D. (1998). *Visual tools and software*. (1998). Lyme, NH: Designs for Thinking (companion to ASCD Visual Tools books; 90 minutes; includes audiotape and guide).

Hyerle, D. (Presenter). (2000). *Visual tools: From graphic organizers to thinking maps*. Sandy, UT: Video Journal of Education. (Elementary and Secondary Editions: videos, audiotapes, and guides.)

Margulies, N. (1993). *Maps, mindscapes, and more*. Tucson, AZ: Zephyr Press.

Software

Thinking Maps®: Technology for learning. (1998). Raleigh, NC: Innovative Learning Group.

Inspiration Software®. (1998). Portland, OR: Inspiration Software, Inc.

MacMapper Software. (1995). Jamaica, NY: St. John's University.

Web Sites

www.graphic.org
www.inspiration.com
www.mapthemind.com
www.mindmanager.com
www.thinkingmaps.com

Index

Note: An f after a page number indicates a figure on that page.

About the Author

David Hyerle is an independent consultant working with whole schools and districts for long-term change over multiple years. He is also a keynote speaker, researcher, and writer in the fields of visual tools, critical thinking, and systemic change. He has authored numerous books and articles, as well as co-produced videos and software based on visual tools. In 1988 he developed the Thinking Maps® language of visual tools, which is now used in nearly 1,000 whole schools worldwide. Most recently, David has been working in New Zealand, Singapore, Canada, and other locales to follow his interest in applying Thinking Maps across cultures. He continues his work as a board member for Educators for Social Responsibility, a nonprofit organization working with schools in the areas of conflict resolution, social and emotional intelligence, and violence prevention. He lives near the White Mountains in New Hampshire with his wife Sara and son Alex, and may be reached through his e-mail address (designs.thinking@valley.net) and Web site (www.mapthemind.com).

Related ASCD Resources

Print Products

Dimensions of Learning Teachers' Manual, 2nd Edition (#197133) by Robert J. Marzano, Debra Pickering, and others

Tools for Learning: A Guide for Teaching Study Skills (#61190086) by M. D. Gall, Joyce P. Gall, Dennis R. Jacobsen, and Terry L. Bullock

Understanding by Design (#198199) by Grant Wiggins and Jay McTighe

The Understanding by Design Handbook (#199030) by Jay McTighe and Grant Wiggins

Visual Tools for Constructing Knowledge (#196072) by David Hyerle.

Videotapes

The Brain and Early Childhood (two tapes, #400054).

The Brain and Learning (four tapes, #498062).

The Brain and Reading (three tapes, #499207).

How to Use Graphic Organizers to Promote Student Thinking (#499048), Tape 6 of the "How To" Series.

Concept Definition Map (#499262), Tape 5 of The Lesson Collection Video Series: Reading Strategies.

ASCD product numbers for the above products are noted in parentheses. For additional information, visit us on the World Wide Web (http://www.ascd.org), send an e-mail message to member@ascd.org, call the ASCD Service Center (1-800-933-ASCD or 703-578-9600, then press 2), send a fax to 703-575-5400, or write to Information Services, ASCD, 1703 N. Beauregard St., Alexandria, VA 22311-1714 USA.